I0540438

Chronicles of Hope

HOW GOD STILL ANSWERS PRAYER
IN MIRACULOUS WAYS UNDER
IMPOSSIBLE CIRCUMSTANCES

Teresa Nell Conkel

Chronicles of Hope: How God Still Answers Prayer in Miraculous Ways Under Impossible Circumstances

Copyright © 2025 by Teresa Nell Conkel

Scripture taken from the King James Version (KJV) is in the public domain.

Scripture quotations marked (NKJV) are taken from the New King James Version®. Copyright © 1982 by Thomas Nelson. Used by permission. All rights reserved.

Scripture quotations marked (NIV) are taken from the Holy Bible, New International Version®, NIV®. Copyright © 1973, 1978, 1984, 2011 by Biblica, Inc.® Used by permission. All rights reserved worldwide.

Scripture quotations marketed (ESV) are from The Holy Bible, English Standard Version® (ESV®), copyright © 2001 by Crossway, a publishing ministry of Good News Publishers. Used by permission. All rights reserved.

Scripture quotations marked (NLT) are taken from the Holy Bible, New Living Translation, copyright © 1996, 2004, 2015 by Tyndale House Foundation. Used by permission of Tyndale House Publishers, Carol Stream, Illinois 60188. All rights reserved.

Scripture quotations marked (NASB) are taken from the New American Standard Bible® (NASB), Copyright © 1960, 1962, 1963, 1968, 1971, 1972, 1973, 1975, 1977, 1995, 2020 by The Lockman Foundation. Used by permission. All rights reserved.

Scripture quotations marked (AMP) are taken from the Amplified® Bible, Copyright © 1954, 1958, 1962, 1964, 1965, 1987 by The Lockman Foundation. Used by permission. All rights reserved.

The Holy Bible, Berean Standard Bible (BSB), produced in cooperation with Bible Hub, Discovery Bible, OpenBible.com, and the Berean Bible Translation Committee. This text of God's Word has been dedicated to the public domain.

Scripture quotations marked (CEV) are from the Contemporary English Version Copyright © 1991, 1992, 1995 by American Bible Society. Used by Permission.

Scripture is taken from GOD'S WORD®. © 1995, 2003, 2013, 2014, 2019, 2020 by God's Word to the Nations Mission Society. Used by permission.

All rights reserved. No portion of this publication may be reproduced, stored in a retrieval system, or transmitted in any form by any means—electronic, mechanical, photocopying, recording, or any other—without prior permission from the author.

ISBN: 979-8-218-67161-7

Design and publishing services by wildcreativepublishing.com

"Give ear my people, to my law; incline your ears to the words of my mouth. I will open my mouth in a parable; I will utter dark sayings of old: Which we have heard and known, and our fathers have told us. We will not hide them from their children, showing to the generation to come the praises of the Lord and his strength, and his wonderful works that he hath done...that they should make them known to their children...that they may set their hope in God and not forget the works of God, but keep his commandments."

Psalm 78: 1-7 (KJV)

Dedication

This book is dedicated to Jeanene, my spiritual mother, teacher, mentor, friend, and true champion of the faith.

Contents

Introduction

AT THE AGE of six, there was a hunger and longing within me to know the Lord. Although my mother (who was divorced) worked arduously to support our family of five, going to church was not a priority. Actually, it was non-existent. We got a taste of religion when a bus would pick my sisters and me up to go to church, but that was short-lived. Regardless of the circumstances, I found the Lord, invited Him into my heart, and was filled with the baptism of the Holy Spirit by the age of 13.

The trajectory of my life changed from that moment on, and an incredible journey with the Lord began. My future was rewritten. Instead of walking down a path of hopelessness (of which I believe the end result would have led to agnosticism) I began a relationship with the God of the Universe. As you read through *Chronicles of Hope*, you'll see where Father God intervenes, provides, and fills the void of an earthly father time and time again. The Lord's supernatural, unusual, (and sometimes) miraculous answers to prayer, restoration, and hope are woven within each chapter like the threads in a tapestry.

May the Lord reveal Himself to you in a greater measure as you begin to relate to family members, identify with relationships, and feel the plethora of emotions that come in times of tragedy as well as triumph. Also, may He weave a beautiful tapestry of hope in your heart with the turn of each page.

CHAPTER 1

———

Finding My Faith

GROWING UP

I was born in Fort Worth, Texas, in 1959, the fourth and last of my mother's children. I was raised by a single mother with the help of my mother's parents whom we fondly called Nanny and Daddy D. My parents divorced when I was very little – so young, in fact, that I don't remember a time when my father lived with us. But I know he did because I have the old pictures and home movies of vacations and Christmas, and he's there. He moved us to California when I was about three, but I don't remember the move. I do remember the beautiful weather and Redondo beach. We moved back to Texas a few years later, and he wasn't there. He stayed in California and eventually remarried.

Relatives and friends started referring to our family of five as "Nell and the kids," which included my mother, brother, 2 sisters, and me. We were not a church-going family, but memories of VBS or church camp at Lake Texoma with my two sisters come to mind when I think of my childhood. There was also a brief period when I was six that I was picked up by a white-painted school bus, which took me and my sisters to church. Once on the bus, we joined other kids (whose parents were apparently not keen on going to church either) and belted out in quasi-unison, "I've got the joy, joy, joy, down in my heart … and if the devil doesn't like it, he can sit on a tack – Ouch!" Needless to say, the church bus experience was short-lived. For reasons unbeknownst to me, it stopped picking us up.

I must have missed going, although I don't remember anything about it. One Sunday morning, I woke Mother up and asked her to take me to church. With eyes still closed, she didn't hesitate to say that in order to go to church you have to have money (for the offering, I suppose). So, I eagerly scrounged up any loose change from around the house, and then ran back to her bedroom to inform her that I had the money. "Can we go to church now?" I asked. She just rolled over, continued sleeping, and that was that.

Sometime later, she asked why I wanted to go to church. I blurted out, "To pray!" I really don't know exactly why I said that except I just wanted to go. She was quick to answer back, saying something to the effect of, "The only time people pray is when someone dies." Church became a mute issue for several years after that.

GETTING SAVED

In the early '70s, the Hippie movement was still in full swing. Teenagers were "turning on (to drugs), tuning in, and dropping out (of school)" as Timothy Leary, a leader during that era would say. One of my cousins was living the mantra so much so, that after quitting high school, she came to live with relatives in our area. It was during this time that she was saved. Her demeanor changed for the better. She was no longer using drugs, and that alone got my attention. It was not long before she moved back to her small home-town in East Texas.

It was the week of Easter, 1972 that I had the choice of either visiting my best friend and former neighbor, or accept an invitation to visit my cousin, who had become very enthusiastic about her newly-found faith. I chose the latter out of curiosity.

We went to the Wednesday night service at my cousin's small Assembly of God church. It was unlike anything I had ever experienced. All the parishioners were engaged and enthusiastic in their worship, and I wanted what they had. By the time Easter Sunday came, I was ready to meet the Jesus they wholeheartedly worshipped. When the preacher gave the altar call for salvation, I was ready. My cousin escorted me to the front, where I received the Lord as my personal savior.

Her small church was in Naples, Texas, a few hours away from Fort Worth, and was not feasible to attend on a weekly basis. When I started looking for something local, I used her AG church as my template. The church in Naples was different from anything I'd ever experienced. It was alive–perhaps a bit on the wild side, but the congregants had a passion in their worship that I had never seen before.

They sang, clapped, shouted, and wept during worship. Between songs, they mumbled and sometimes shouted in languages I didn't understand. I didn't comprehend their strange language. Regardless, whatever they were saying was spoken with gusto! Since I couldn't find an AG church in our suburb, my cousin advised me to look for a Pentecostal church.

Pentecostal or AG, it didn't matter to me. I just wanted to be around people who had that passion and zeal for the Lord like they did at my cousin's church. So, how does one go about finding such a church? I let my fingers "do the walking" through the Yellow Pages section of the phone book. That was the information technology of our day, before the invention of Google or the internet.

I prayed and then scanned the Pages for a local Pentecostal church. Precious Faith Temple (PFT) in Lake Worth jumped off the page. From that moment on, I started planning a visit for that church's next Sunday morning service. I called the church for service time(s) and directions. Fortunately, someone was at church to answer the phone, so I was given all the info I needed.

By this time, all my siblings were driving, so coming up with a buck for gas money in exchange for transportation was a no brainer. I don't remember exactly who took me and picked me up, but one of them took the bait.

I WASN'T STOPPED FROM GOING TO CHURCH UNTIL …

Mother and my grandparents identified themselves as Christians, as opposed to being Atheists, I suppose. They were not practicing Christians and not involved in church. They did not pray, nor were they associated with other believers. Regardless, we rarely donned the door of any church. That was not a part of our lives; however, I wasn't prevented from going. By this time, I was 13. Mother didn't care whether or not I went to church, just as long as she didn't have to go. Also, since all my siblings were driving, at least one of them could drop me off or pick me up at the front door.

That first Sunday morning service at PFT was pretty mild in comparison to the evening service; it was wild! There was a guest preacher-evangelist leading the service that night. He really fired up the congregation. After we sang endless verses and choruses of sometimes the same hymn, the evangelist gave an altar call. He invited any and all to come up front for prayer, healing, and any and all other needs. Since I knew no one in the congregation, I sat at the end of a pew alone, just watching all the goings-on.

A few minutes later, a sweet, middle-aged pregnant woman came over and sat by me. She leaned over and spoke to me like she knew my inner thoughts. I later learned that was a Word of Knowledge, which is a gift spoken of in the New Testament. It is when the Holy Spirit "reads your mail" and reveals something about you to someone who would not know it otherwise. 1 Corinthians 12 speaks about such gifts of the Spirit in detail.

The Word she spoke was, "The Lord shows me you have been seeking a gift from Him." Startled by what she said, I replied, "No, I haven't!" She then scooted away from me, moving more to the center of the pew. I lied. I had been seeking the baptism of the Holy Ghost as I wanted that funny, but exuberant language, too. Why I rejected what she said, I don't know, but her Word was spot on. After all, that's the whole reason I searched for this church in the first place! What was I thinking?

A few minutes later, I went over and sat next to her. Very sheepishly, I told her I had been wanting to receive the Holy Ghost (Holy Ghost and Holy Spirit mean the same thing, but the people I'd been around introduced Him as the Holy Ghost). She graciously escorted me to the altar – then the REAL fireworks began, in the Spirit, that is!

As I knelt down at the altar, I began to raise my hands. The pastor and the lady who had walked me to the altar (and every other lady there that night) laid their hands on my head or shoulders. Suddenly, I became the center of attention. The service was not going to end until I was filled with the Holy Ghost. By now, church exceeded its scheduled dismissal time.

In the meantime, Mother, who was waiting in the church parking lot to pick me up, ended up going back home. Later on, when I asked her why she didn't come in the sanctuary to get me, she told me it was "too loud" and she could hear the noise from outside. Personally, I think she was too scared to go in. In any event, the pastor and his wife ended up taking me home.

The pastor escorted me to the door and apologized to Mom for the service going so late. Mother was cordial to him as she accepted his apology. Then she shut the door and told me that I was never going back to THAT church again. Obviously, she was angry, but I didn't care. I was floating on cloud nine as I had finally been baptized in the Holy Spirit.

FALLING ROCKS

From the moment Mother told me I couldn't go back to the church, things were tense between us. Church attendance was off the table. She thought I'd lost my mind and that PFT was some sort of cult. She didn't understand any of it, and conveyed her dismay to my grandparents.

When my cousin got saved and filled with the Spirit, they were baffled. They were OK with the "getting saved" part but drew the line on the "getting filled with Spirit" aspect. In their minds, receiving the baptism of the Holy Spirit was going too far. So, when I came home talking about my experience, they thought I had gone off the deep end. My family thought Pentecostal people were fanatics, and Nanny even referred to them as "Holy Rollers." (As long as I've been involved with the charismatic church, I've yet to see anyone roll around on the floor.)

I called the church office at some point to tell them what was going on at home. The call took place while Mom was at work and my siblings were not home or they would have tattled on me. This was before cell phones and caller ID, and the only phone in the house, which was an old rotary phone, had little to no extension cord.

The phone was located in a narrow hallway, and you could pretty much hear all phone conversations in any room in the house. That's why I had to be very stealthy and contact the church incognito. At age 13, it was most likely I was home alone anyway. My brother had already moved out, and the sisters were probably working summer jobs, or hanging out at the lake with friends.

We lived in a small A-Frame house in West Fort Worth, not too far from military base housing. When my brother moved out, one sister moved in to his old room. This meant that I now shared a bedroom with my other sister. My siblings and I get along fine now, and I love all of them and their families with all my heart, but that was not necessarily the case when we were growing up.

We were all polar opposites in every aspect of the term and constantly "fought and scratched," as Nanny used to say, like cats and dogs. I was a bit meticulous about keeping my side of the room clean while my new roommate went the science route, growing mold on discarded fast food under a dark bed.

In the early '70s, the décor of a true hippie teenager's bedroom consisted of a Black Light (ultraviolet light) and fluorescent posters. Over my bed hung a light-weight, bright orange fish net which spanned the width and length of the bed. Placed ever so carefully in the net were a variety of sea coral, shells, rocks, and a small conch shell or two – all painted in an array of florescent colors. The whole conglomeration was hung from the ceiling with a few flat-head thumb tacks. Obviously, the teenage female design team concluded this was the way to mount all that stuff. So much for high school physics!

One Friday afternoon, Mother came home from work and was in a hurry to get to her lake house, which she fondly called the Cabin, in Lindale. It was a few hours away, and she was anxious to get on the road in order to be there before dark. She would meet up with her best friend, Sue, on the east side of Fort Worth at a specific time to carpool to the lake. Time was of the essence.

Mother was fit to be tied when she discovered my sister had not done any of her chores that day, one of which involved laundry. This faux pas delayed Mother's rendezvous. Heads were going to roll and my sister, who had dropped the ball, got in trouble. Assuming that I had tattled on her for not doing the laundry, my sister found me in the bedroom and took her frustrations out on me. The funny thing is I had not tattled on her.

It was obvious to Mom that she had not done her job(s). My sister grabbed some dirty laundry, either a towel or a pair of jeans, that was laying on the floor. She aimed to swat me, but instead hit the net above, pulling it and its contents away from the ceiling.

Everything came crashing down, and my scalp got caught in the downfall. After I let out a blood-curdling scream, Mother quickly ran to our room, gasped and ushered me to the bathroom, grabbing some towels along the way. Some debris was embedded in my scalp, mixed with blood and tangled hair. The more Mother tried to stop the bleeding, the more it hurt, and the more I cried. During all this mayhem, the culprit stealthily made her exit from the scene of the crime and, from that point on, was nowhere to be found.

I don't know why I wasn't taken to the emergency room. (One time when we were living in California, I was taken to the emergency room when my finger got shut in the car door. Why I wasn't taken to the hospital for this, I'll never know.) She grabbed more towels and daubed my head, and everywhere she daubed, there was more blood.

As she retrieved debris, she pulled my hair, which made it hurt even more. Some of the smaller pieces even went deeper into the wounds after she daubed my scalp. Every so often, she let out a little sigh under her breath. I'm sure what she was dealing with was unsightly, but all I knew was that I was in pain.

To make matters worse, I had long, heavy hair, which exacerbated the problem. On top of all that, I had the worst headache of my life. I don't know which felt worse, the injuries or the headache. It was a toss-up.

Finally, Mother got on the phone to Nanny to either get medical advice or a home remedy. While on the phone, she handed me the cloth to daub my own injuries. After she got off the phone, I asked her if I could call the church to have them pray for God to heal my head. Reluctantly, she let me call, which was a miracle within itself.

It was early evening by now, and neither of us expected anyone to be at the church at that time of day, especially on a Friday. Whether I left a message with an answering service or if someone actually picked up the phone, I don't remember. But somewhere in the course of all the mayhem, I did actually talk to the pastor, Brother Terry, who then requested to speak to my mother.

Later on, I found out that the pastor was often at church on Friday evenings to pray before Sunday's service. Mother didn't really want to talk to him, but I gave the phone to her anyway. Their conversation was brief, but cordial. There was a moment of silence while she listened to what he had to say, then she ended the conversation with, "Thank you. Goodbye."

I think Brother Terry might have led her in prayer over the phone or, at the very least, said he would pray. I don't know how Mother received all that, but at least she didn't hang up on him.

A LITTLE CHILD SHALL LEAD THEM

I woke up feeling okay the next morning after the "falling rocks" incident. I don't remember waking up feeling instantly or miraculously healed, but I was better. After a bit, I ran my fingers over my scalp to feel the lacerations and could not feel anything but smooth skin—no cuts or sores, nothing but perfectly normal skin on my scalp.

I went to find Mother to have her examine my wounds. Since I couldn't see my scalp, I had no idea what it had looked like the night before. However, I could feel it with my fingertips, and there was a notable difference. My head didn't feel sore, and now it didn't hurt. I no longer had a throbbing headache. Mother, however, knew exactly what it looked like as she had seen it all—the blood, debris, cuts, everything. I bent my head over for her to examine it, and then told her that I thought God had healed my head. She simultaneously sighed and rolled her eyes as she thought I had become delusional from the head trauma.

She then re-examined the same spots where she had seen the wounds less than 24 hours before. As gently as possible, she parted small sections of hair on my scalp for what seemed to be an eternity. Every once in a while, she'd let out a "Huh!" then continue to examine more sections of hair.

After a while, she stopped and called Nanny on the phone. She told her how "the preacher at Tessie's church" (Tessie is my nickname) had prayed, and how yesterday, she had doctored multiple cuts on my head, but those cuts were not there today. The Lord had healed my head. God had answered prayer in a miraculous way. Mother went from being the antagonist to the evangelist in a nano second.

After a while, my grandparents made their way to our house. By that time, I felt a bit like the side show at a circus, as my head was on display for all to see. "Look at this, Mother!" she said to Nanny. Daddy D came over, equipped with his thick-rimmed reading glasses, glanced over Nanny's shoulders and let out a soft, "Well, I'll be!" In thorough examination mode, Mother pointed out the places where she had seen the injuries first-hand the night before. Now, there were no scars.

The next day, Sunday morning, all three of them went with me to the Pentecostal church. I was beaming with pride as my family walked into church with me. After they were seated, I made my way to find Brother Terry, to show him the miracle God had done with my head.

The Lord must have really touched Nanny. Through it all, she kept saying "… a little child shall lead them." (Isaiah 11:6 KJV)

CHAPTER 2

Hope in the Small Things

A BOYFRIEND, A CAR, AND AN ANSWER TO PRAYER

It's not uncommon for teenagers to inherit the oldest vehicle in the family after getting their driver's licenses. I was no exception. My siblings had inherited an old blue '55 Buick Century, which was appropriately nicknamed, "The War Wagon." It looked like a big two-toned tank driving down the road.

The old Buick would be considered a classic today, but back in the '70s it was embarrassing to drive it or even ride in it. Regardless, it was either that or have no transportation at all. Thankfully, the old Buick went to be with the Lord before it was passed down to me, so I inherited my sister's gray '62 Chevy Nova.

In the meantime, both of my sisters were able to upgrade to the newest and most popular compact car of the day, the Ford Pinto. Each purchased their own, with Mother co-signing for one of the Pintos. Unfortunately, she ended up getting stuck with that car and the remaining payments.

Although it was the prettiest and newest car in the family, Mother hated driving it. Vinyl seats, no A/C, and a standard transmission didn't suit her at all. Insufficient leg room also didn't fit my mother's tall stature.

The Pinto sat idle in front of our house for weeks on end. She tried to sell it, even advertising for someone to take up the payments just to get rid of it. I liked the car, so I started praying to get it, and Nanny started agreeing in prayer with me.

Little did I know that God was going to use my mother's long-standing boyfriend Al to answer my prayer. Al was a "Good time Charlie" to say the least. Mother couldn't live with him, but she couldn't live without him either. He was a big man, a heavy-set guy who stood about 6' 4", had jet black hair, and a boisterous personality. He excelled at sports and games of all sorts.

A kid at heart, he never grew up and only held down a job for the sole purpose of funding his love for drinking and entertainment. He would give you the shirt off his back while simultaneously walking over your carefully planted flowers in the front yard. When given a simple home repair task, he would leave things in worse shape than originally found.

One time he bought my mother a set of thick, milk white, state-of-the-art bakeware. With the excitement of a child opening a gift at Christmas, he unpacked the box, setting a few pieces of the cookware on the portable dishwasher. In his booming voice, he recited to Mom the sales pitch that sealed the deal for him: The bakeware was unbreakable.

Before we knew it, he set out to prove his point by throwing one of the pieces (the prettiest piece – as my mother later recalled) on the kitchen floor where it shattered into a million pieces. I gasped, and Mother yelled as we both looked on in horror. My sister had the best reaction of all as she handed him another dish and said, "Here! Try another one!" That was Al.

He drove an old, green car that was always in disrepair. One time he let his gas tank run dry. With several failed attempts to get the car to the nearest service station, he poured kerosene into the tank as a substitute for fuel. The short-term solution made the car backfire and sputter to no end. It was quite a sight to see. Needless to say, the car was never the same after that, so my mother let him drive the Pinto.

He wrecked the Pinto within a few weeks, damaging the front driver's side, which was later repaired. However, upon impact, he held on to the steering wheel, and in doing so, he pulled the wheel to the left with such force that it could not be totally straightened after that. It was drivable, but the steering wheel remained left of center for the rest of the car's life.

Mother desperately tried to sell the car again after the wreck; she just wanted someone to take it off her hands. All attempts were futile. No one wanted to take up payments on a car that had been through a wreck and had an off-center steering wheel.

Even though she hated it, Mother started driving the Pinto again, as it was still the newest car. After all, she was paying for it. I was still driving her old Chevy at the time. Her Chevy was like driving a big white boat, but it did have A/C. Also, beggars can't be choosers, and I needed dependable transportation to get to and from school and work.

Mother finally threw in the towel and wanted her Chevy with A/C back. Driving in rush-hour traffic in a car with no A/C in the Texas summer heat became too much for her. She didn't want the Pinto, couldn't get rid of it, didn't want Al to drive it, so I got it by default. Other than the steering wheel being off center, the Pinto drove just fine. I ended up driving that car for a few years.

Through a series of unexpected events, the Lord answered our prayers for the Pinto. This ended up being a defining moment in my walk with the Lord, as I now began to see God as my loving, caring Father and provider. My prayer life and faith to believe God increased exponentially. Also, Nanny got to witness God's faithfulness once more. God moves in mysterious ways.

SEEING THE LORD

Jeanene was a prophet, Bible teacher, intercessor, confidant, and dear friend. I considered her my spiritual mother. Jeanene and I had relatives in common, as Nanny's sister-in-law was Jeanene's aunt. When my cousin moved from Fort Worth to Dallas to live with her other relatives, it was Jeanene and her mother (whom we fondly called Aunt Reba) that led my cousin to the Lord.

My cousin would take me with her to visit Jeanene when traveling through Dallas on the way to East Texas. Our visits usually consisted of a meal, followed by a brief Bible study and prayer. Although we had a cousin in common, Jeanene and I were not blood relatives. She really became my spiritual mother when I began attending a weekly Bible study in her home my freshman year in college.

Jeanene had a walk with the Lord that would provoke anyone to "Spiritual Jealousy." I was in awe of how she talked and prayed to the Lord, as if He were in the room. Jesus was her constant companion and best friend. She had encounters with Him all the time, as the Lord gifted her with spiritual dreams and visions. Visitations from the Lord were commonplace with her.

I wanted to experience these extraordinary encounters, too. One time after she shared one of her encounters with the Lord, I asked her to pray that I would see Jesus in the same way she did. She smiled and said that she would pray the Lord would show Himself in a tangible way to me. Not long after that, I had an unusual experience after I fell asleep one night. In a dreamlike state, I felt myself ascending up in a white cloud. At the time, I didn't know where I was going. I felt myself just gently floating upward.

The next thing I knew, I was looking directly into some-one's eye, a brilliant eye, where flames of fire were shooting out of it. It was powerful and frightening all at the same time! In the split second after that, there was a hand lifting me up close to the person with the fiery eye. It was the nail scarred hand of the Lord Jesus Himself bringing me closer to Him. Although our meeting was brief, and I can't remember what I said to Him, I will never forget the three words He spoke to me: "Have More Compassion." His words left me speechless.

Immediately, I felt myself descending through the white clouds, and back into my body. It was as if I were salt being poured into a salt shaker. In my mind, I was screaming, "NO!! I don't want to go! Let me stay with you, Lord!" However, He would not let me stay - I had to come back.

This brief encounter was just a glimpse of the glory that lies ahead and how wonderful it was. If there were ever a question of the Lord's existence, this visitation erased all doubt. It was a game changer which deepened my faith and walk with Him.

"His head and his hairs were white like wool, as white as snow; and his eyes were as a flame of fire." (Revelation 1:14 KJV)

SEANCES AND OUIJA BOARDS

When I was a child, and before I had a relationship with the Lord, I played on a Ouija board with Mother and my sisters. Mother had one when she was growing up, so she bought one for us as well. I remember how we placed our fingers on the plastic triangle device that hovered over letters, which spelled words in response to the innocent questions it was asked. The more it answered our questions, the more intrigued we became.

Seances were something else we delved into once or twice, inviting school or neighborhood kids to summon up the dearly departed, such as George Washington or Abraham Lincoln. Sitting in a circle around a lighted candle in a dark bedroom seemed like harmless fun. I admit I was scared, but curious, to hear from the ghost of a former president or two.

Thankfully, seances came to an abrupt end when someone called on a dead President to manifest by showing us a tangible sign of his presence in the room. Without skipping a beat, one of the teenagers in the room threw a hairbrush against the wall. The loud thump sent everyone screaming as they ran out of the room. Needless to say, we never did another séance after that.

The summer after I got saved, I began to watch the 700 Club. At the time, the show's format was like that of the Tonight Show with various guests. At one point in the broadcast, the host, Pat Robertson, would hone in and minister on a specific topic. Pat's area of ministry on the show I was watching that day focused on the occult. He revealed that dabbling in such things as Ouija boards and seances, although they seem innocent, opens the door to demonic activity. Even tarot cards were off the table, so to speak. He told us we needed to get rid of such things, and renounce any association with the practice thereof.

I felt the conviction of the Lord to find and get rid of the Ouija board. Immediately, I scavenged through our stack of games in a closet and found it. I couldn't burn it as Pat had suggested, but I did break it into as many pieces as possible. Timing for the garbage pickup couldn't have worked out better. No sooner had I pitched the broken pieces in the trash, here came the garbage truck down the alley.

The board had not been used in a few years, so no one ever knew it was gone. I was relieved more than anything that it was out of the house, as my eyes had been opened to the spiritualism attached to the board. It did cross my mind that I would be punished if my mother ever found out; however, it was more important to get rid of it and face the consequences. I knew it was the right thing to do.

"Get up, sanctify the people, and say, 'Sanctify yourselves for tomorrow, because thus says the Lord God of Israel:

There is an accursed thing in your midst, O Israel; you cannot stand before your enemies until you take away the accursed thing from among you.'" (Joshua 7:13 NKJV)

CHAPTER 3

Hope for the Future

SHE WANTED A MUSICIAN IN THE FAMILY-BUT NOT REALLY

When we were in elementary school, my siblings and I began taking instrumental music lessons. My brother and oldest sister took accordion lessons, thanks to Lawrence Welk, who intermittently played the accordion along with the LW orchestra on his popular TV show. My other sister started piano lessons not long after we moved back to Texas. I had no choice but to tag along with Mother to my sister's lessons. She took from an elderly woman whose home was filled with old furniture and antiques.

The old piano fit right in with that decor. Mother and I sat in some sort of formal living room that was adjacent to the piano room. With the door between the rooms always open, we heard every right (and wrong) note, every correction, and directions as to what to practice for the next lesson.

Although my sister was not motivated to practice, I was. When we got home from her lessons, I would head to the piano to pick out the tunes I'd just heard. This went on for a while, until Mother finally had me show the piano teacher what I was doing. Shortly after that, I began taking lessons. Although my passion for music began with the piano, it continued through singing in choir, and playing flute in both high school band and orchestra. Music was and still is my passion.

When I was 15, my main summer job was babysitting. One job that lasted a few weeks involved watching 2 young girls. They loved playing "school." They were the students; I was the teacher. As we were playing, the Lord whispered in my ear, "One day you will be a teacher of music." I never forgot those words as that was when the Lord revealed my destiny. I did not share this with anyone but kept it a secret instead.

My family already thought I was strange because I was Pentecostal, so I learned to not tell them anything that the Lord had spoken to me. I would be either laughed at or ignored. Sometimes it is just better to not cast your pearls before the swine, as scripture says. Stay silent, and let the Lord fulfill His Word - even if it takes time. In my case, it took several years for this prophecy to come to pass.

Before I knew it, I was a senior in high school with graduation in sight. I needed to finalize decisions about the future. I knew what the Lord had spoken, but was clueless as to how to get there. Mother allowed me to entertain the idea of going to college, but it was never her intention for me to actually go.

She couldn't afford to pay any college tuition, and I certainly didn't have the funds. Nevertheless, I applied and was accepted into a few local and out of town colleges. I wanted to pursue a career in music. Mother always wanted at least one of us to be a musician, which only meant being competent in singing or playing an instrument. It was never her vision for any of us to pursue music as a career. She thought being a musician was frivolous, and we couldn't make a living at it.

Mother had just gotten rehired at General Dynamics (GD), after having been jobless for a while. She had been fired from a small construction company while going through cancer treatment, so my aspirations for college were the last thing on her mind. Her goal was for me to work full-time, and take a night class or two as I could afford it. That was her answer, end of story. That, however, was not the plan God had for me. I knew what the Lord had spoken years before about being a music teacher. Furthermore, I had no desire, nor was I qualified, to work at GD.

In the meantime, I kept walking forward in faith, even though I didn't know where I was going or how I was going to get there. A friend from choir and I even went so far as to plan on reserving a dorm room at Texas Tech. Both of us had received our letters of acceptance; however, when the time came to put down the dorm room deposit, I didn't have peace nor the money.

It was springtime by now, and time was ticking away. With no money and no direction, I sought the Lord and reminded Him of His word to me when I was 15, of becoming a music teacher. Let me tell you, God needs no reminders. Although I didn't see it at the time, the Lord was working behind the scenes all along, to fulfill His Word. He was on it, years before I graduated from high school.

"For I know the plans I have for you, declares the Lord, plans to prosper you and not to harm you, plans to give you hope and a future." (Jeremiah 29:11 NIV)

THE BUS STOPS HERE

As far back as I can remember, I loved hearing Texas Christian University's Concert Chorale perform. It was my dream to go to college there and sing with the Chorale; however, TCU is a private university which meant high tuition. That was just a pipe dream, and I didn't give any serious thought of actually going there due to the cost.

It was now April, and graduation was not far off. Reality hit and the writing was on the wall. The truth of the matter was I could not afford to go to college, and I needed to stop kidding myself. Classmates were finalizing their college plans, discussing dorm life, contemplating what classes to take, while I was having to die, so to speak, to my college dreams. I had to lay it down at the Lord's feet and let it go. It wasn't long after I did this that the Lord revealed His plan to me in a dream.

One night I dreamed that I was riding in a yellow school bus. As the bus came to a stop, the door opened and I got out. The driver dropped me off right in front of Ed Landreth auditorium, which was the main music building on the TCU campus. As the door closed behind me, the bus drove off, leaving me alone in front of the building. Although the dream was short, it was to the point.

After I woke up, the Lord spoke to my heart and said, "I will provide." Since TCU was not far from home, it was a no brainer to just drive to the campus to pick up the required paperwork for admission. This must have expedited the process, as I was accepted fairly quickly. Before I knew it, I was auditioning for music professors, which was a requirement for majoring in music.

My first audition involved playing flute for the band director. Although the audition went well, that professor really didn't give me the time of day. Disappointed, I went home and poured out my frustrations before the Lord. God was quick to respond. I was going the right direction, but the wrong discipline. Perhaps my field of study should be voice instead of flute.

The next week, I was auditioning in front of three vocal/choral music professors, one of which was the Concert Chorale director. All went well, and I was accepted into the vocal music program. However, it would all be for naught if the money wasn't there.

At the end of the audition, the topic of finances came up. After a brief discussion about my tuition concerns, one of the professors kindly asked me to wait outside the door. The professors who remained in the room discussed the situation at hand. She had apparently made a phone call to the Financial Aid office while I was waiting in the wings.

As soon as I was summoned to go back into the room, one of the professors handed me a note with the name and location of a Financial Aid advisor on campus—who was expecting me. Without hesitation, I drove to the Office of Financial Aid before it closed for the weekend.

"A man's heart plans his way, but the Lord directs his steps." (Proverbs 16:9 NKJV)

A PROMISE MADE, A PROMISE KEPT

I went home, excited to tell Mom all that had transpired during the audition. Then, I handed her the stack of financial aid forms. It was Friday afternoon, and she was in a hurry to get to the Cabin for the weekend. Looking through paperwork was the last thing on her mind. To get me off her back, she said she'd look at it upon her return from the Cabin, but I wasn't going to hold my breath. She was already perturbed that I still had my sights set on college after graduation, instead of working full-time. The favorable audition, along with handing her a plethora of financial aid forms, exacerbated the tension between us.

After she left, I went to my room and prayed until God gave me peace over the whole situation. Perhaps it was wrong timing on my part to present financial aid papers to her as she was leaving for the weekend. In any event, the Lord reminded me of the "Bus" dream and His promise of provision.

Now, it all boiled down to walking by faith and letting the Lord work it out. I didn't know what to expect when she returned from the Cabin the following Sunday, but I knew better than to nag her. Sometimes God not only requires us to wait but to be silent.

After she came home from the Cabin and unwound a bit, she asked to see the paperwork. That alone was an answer to prayer. Along with some personal information, the forms required income verification and tax returns from previous years, which I knew nothing about. Now the ball was in her court. The next answer to prayer took place when Mother was proactive in completing the forms. She is the one who contacted Financial Aid to make sure every "T" had been crossed, every "I" dotted, and all documents required of us were ready for submission.

As it turned out, Mother's previous extended time of unemployment became the determining factor in the amount of financial aid I was awarded. Not only did I receive enough grants and aid to go to college full-time, I was able to live and work on campus. A meal plan was also provided.

I did have to pay back a small college loan, but had no problem paying it off before I got married. God did what He said He would do, and what only He can do. Looking back, I marvel at how every step of getting to college, graduating, and securing my first teaching position was orchestrated by the Lord.

"God is not a man that He should lie, neither the son of man, that He should repent: Has He said, and shall He not do it? Or has He spoken, and shall He not make it good?" (Numbers 23:19 KJV)

CHAPTER 4

Hope for Community

A FROG IN THE FOG

In August of 1977, I finally moved into the college dorm. Purple and white served as background for the TCU logo, along with "Go Frogs" and pictures of the Frog mascot. Although I was officially now a Frog, I felt like a tadpole. There is a big difference between being a senior in high school and a freshman in college.

Dorm life was fun, but the adjustment to having a roommate was difficult at times. Choir was always enjoyable, but the rest of my classes were a challenge and required more studying than I'd ever done. I had achieved many accolades in music while in high school, but past achievements didn't matter anymore.

By the first semester of my sophomore year, music theory became my Achilles heel. A soft-spoken, but very knowledgeable grad student named Betsie became my tutor. I was also still attending Jeanene's Bible study once a week in Dallas. The Bible study took place on Mondays, so we would fast on that day. We would always open with prayer requests before study began. Prayer would conclude by declaring John 14:13-14 (KJV): "Whatsoever ye shall ask in my name, that will I do that the Father may be glorified in the Son. If ye shall ask anything in my name, I will do it."

One of my main prayers was asking the Lord to help me through classes, especially theory. Another big request was that I wanted to get connected with a group of believers on campus at TCU, who loved the Lord and were filled with the Spirit. I had never been involved with a group of Christians my age, and desired that kind of fellowship. I didn't know if such a group even existed.

The Bible study consisted of women ages 45 and older, and my little Pentecostal church was filled with married couples and their children. Oddly enough, the answer to prayer for fellowship came through my theory tutor.

One day after a tutoring session, Betsie and I began chatting about religion, religious fellowships on campus in particular. When she invited me to a Friday night fellowship that she and her husband attended, I blew her off as I knew she was Catholic. In an attempt to scare her away, I told her I was Charismatic.

I was taken aback when she responded, "Me, too!" Since she obviously didn't understand the definition of Charismatic, I further expounded by saying, "I speak in tongues." That should have ended the conversation, or so I thought. Then she threw me a curve ball by saying, "We do, too!"

I was dumbfounded! How could one be Catholic and Charismatic simultaneously? It did not make sense! Out of curiosity more than anything else, I accepted her invitation. I made plans to attend this Friday night fellowship, called the Family of God (FOG).

"I WILL POUR OUT MY SPIRIT …"

Other than the time my stepmother took me to Mass, I knew nothing about the Catholic church. At Mass, I recall a man, dressed in white, walking down the center aisle of the sanctuary. As he walked to the front, he slung droplets of water at the congregants on both sides of the aisle. People bowed when he walked past them.

The congregants sat down, kneeled, and stood up sporadically throughout the service. I don't remember much else, other than this was in stark contrast to my Pentecostal church experience. That is what I expected the FOG meeting to be like.

As I arrived, music could be heard from outside the Community Center of the Catholic Church, where the gathering had already started. As I walked through the door, I saw a couple of guitarists leading worship, accompanied by a tambourine player. There might have been an additional singer or two. The guitarists led with zeal as the crowd followed them in singing, "Lord God 3 in 1…"

They sang with instruments, then a cappella, followed again with guitar and tambourine accompaniment. Between the songs, they shouted, "Praise God! Come Holy Spirit!" and people spoke in tongues. Even though the music was unfamiliar to me, the presence of the Holy Spirit resonated within my heart.

The Bible study had previously prayed for me to find a group of Spirit-filled Christians my age that loved the Lord. I never dreamed that God would answer this prayer with a group I didn't know could possibly exist. This clearly showed me that the Lord looks at your heart, not your religion.

In the '60s and '70s, the Lord was pouring out His Spirit simultaneously on both Protestants and Catholics. The Protestants referred to this phenomenon as the Charismatic Movement, while Catholics referred to this outpouring as the Charismatic Renewal. FOG was an ecumenical group, and although the majority were Catholics, it didn't matter. This group was "on fire" for the Lord and sought Him with all their hearts.

God blessed FOG with an abundance of musical talent. During my last semester of college, the group cut an album entitled, "Honor, Wisdom, Glory, and Praise." The album was a compilation of many worship songs composed and arranged exclusively by FOG members. I was involved in this fellowship for several years until I had to move out of town for a job.

The Lord proved Himself faithful through answered prayer many times over during those college years. Several women in the group who had been diagnosed with fertility issues, some to the point of facing hysterectomies, were miraculously healed and able to conceive. Another couples' answer to prayer came through an unexpected adoption.

One day, literally out of nowhere, an attorney called this couple, informing them that a young woman had specifically requested them to be her baby's parents. They had never applied for adopting a child anywhere. After the baby arrived and the legal paperwork completed, the couple took home their newborn. Throughout the years, it has been a joy to see all the babies we prayed for, regardless of how they got here, as adults who now have children of their own.

Many members have moved out of the area due to job changes and to be closer to family, but we manage to keep in touch through social media, internet, and an occasional reunion. I treasure the bonds of friendships formed, even to this day. When I prayed for a Spirit-filled community, God provided more than I could have ever imagined!

"And in the last days it shall be, God declares, that I will pour out my Spirit on all flesh, and your sons and your daughters shall prophesy, and your young men shall see visions, and your old men shall dream dreams." (Acts 2:17 ESV)

CHAPTER 5

Hope for Provision

TRAPPED IN DALLAS

It was supposed to be a fun, long weekend out-of-town. I had just finished my sophomore year at TCU, and had a few days off before summer classes began. We got a late start and couldn't leave until I got off work. My co-traveler's relative lived on the outskirts of Dallas. We drove for about an hour, then camped out at her relative's apartment overnight.

Not long after we arrived, there was a knock at the door. In came two big, burly men, one of them was wearing a Hell's Angels-type jacket. After a few minutes, it became apparent this was a rendezvous that was preplanned. Then, I was escorted to a room where I'd be sleeping. What I didn't know was, I would be trapped in that room for the duration of the night.

There were no cell phones back then, so I couldn't call anyone to come get me. That wouldn't have mattered, because I didn't know where I was anyway. The party in the living room continued from late in the night, until the wee hours in the morning. To make matters worse, the smell of marijuana crept under the door and into my room. Marijuana was not the minor offense it is today. Back in the

'70s, those caught with it were thrown in jail. When I realized what was going on, I started praying for God to get me out of there! I sought God quietly, but as fervently as possible under the circumstances.

Around 2 am, my fear turned to anger, and the Lord gave me the boldness to confront my co-traveler in the living room. She was irritated at me, as I had bothered her and the others at such a late hour. When I told her I wanted to go home, she responded by saying she wasn't going to take me anywhere, as it was too late. Looking back, I wouldn't have wanted her to drive in the state she was in anyway. Then, her relative pointed toward the window to the bus stop at the corner of the property. The relative told me the bus was scheduled to be at the stop around 5 am.

I packed my bags and bided my time until I could make it out to the bus stop, although it was still pitch-black outside. Crying and scared, I prayed desperately for protection and guidance. Even though I was still clueless as to where I was in Dallas, or what route to take to get back to Fort Worth, one thing I did know: I was determined to get back home.

A few minutes before the bus was scheduled to arrive, an older gentleman walked up to the bus stop to wait as well. He was dressed in a suit and tie, had glasses, and wore a Fedora hat like coach Tom Landry used to wear. I must admit, I was scared, but he kept his distance, standing about six feet away. Then out of the blue, he asked, "Are you lost?" What an odd question coming from a perfect stranger! Nevertheless, I answered, telling him I needed to get back to Fort Worth.

He told me which bus to catch that would get me to downtown Dallas. From there, I could take another bus to downtown Fort Worth. After I thanked the kind gentleman, something bizarre happened: Instead of waiting for his bus, he turned, walked away, and disappeared into the dark.

With all my heart, I believe this was an angel that had taken on human form, who was sent from God to guide me home. "Do not forget to show hospitality to strangers, for by so doing some people have shown hospitality to angels without knowing it." (Hebrews 13:2 NIV). Exhaustion turned to exhilaration, as the reality of what had just taken place set in.

The sun began to rise and people started to slowly gather at the bus stop. Sure enough, the bus that went to the Greyhound downtown Dallas terminal came, just as I was told. I was able to take that bus to downtown Dallas, and from there, caught the bus to downtown Fort Worth. After I arrived at the Fort Worth terminal, I called a friend who picked me up and took me home.

"When I was in deep trouble, I searched for the Lord. All night long I prayed, with hands lifted toward heaven, but my soul was not comforted…You are the God of great wonders! You demonstrate your awesome power among the nation." (Psalm 77:2, 14 NLT)

THE STICK'S ON FIRE

During my summers in college, I worked and took some core classes at the junior college, when possible. Summers in Texas are always hot, but the summer of 1980 (my junior year) was especially brutal. That summer broke all kinds of heat records. North Texas had 69 days of 100+ degree temperatures; 42 of those days were consecutive. That summer, I was a temporary office worker in downtown Fort Worth, which meant driving during rush-hour traffic in the already unbearable heat.

The Pinto had a standard transmission. I must admit, it was fun driving a "stick", but brutal not having air conditioning during the heat wave. Needless to say, I began praying for a car with A/C. In Texas, A/C is pretty much a necessity, especially in the summer. God was about to answer that prayer with a bang!

One Friday evening in July, I parked my car alongside the curb in front of the host home where FOG was meeting. I turned off the engine before getting out of the car, as usual. After taking the key out of the ignition and opening the car door, the engine started up again all by itself. I wasn't too concerned as I had seen this happen before with Daddy D's car, and the problem was fixed. However, the Pinto restarted 3 or 4 times on its own. Then, the car started lurching forward as if it had a mind of its own. It didn't matter that I had my foot on the brake. The next thing I knew, smoke was coming out from all sides of the hood.

One man hurried out of the host home, managing to pop the hood. Heat from the fire was causing the car to self-start and jump forward. Not knowing the severity of the situation, the group's host ran toward my car with a small box of baking soda in one hand and a teaspoon in the other. With intent of extinguishing the fire, she stopped mid-yard, ran back in her house, and called the fire department.

By this time, smoke was billowing out of the hood. Needless to say, a remedy to extinguish the fire was way beyond a teaspoon, or even a box, of baking soda. Within a few minutes, a fire truck arrived on site, and the flames were eventually put out. Even though the fire department responded in a timely manner, the damage had already been done. My car was deemed a total loss.

I must confess, my faith was tested when the Pinto went up in smoke. Instead of having a car with no A/C, I had no car at all! Also, since the car was paid for, I didn't know if it still had full coverage, or just liability. With no transportation and desperate for help, I called upon the Lord, and asked FOG and the Bible study group to pray about the car insurance situation.

Jeanene was not only a great teacher of God's Word, she was a prayer warrior extraordinaire. She taught me to pray with boldness for specific things, and not just pray general prayers. Such was the case when I began praying for another car. With her guidance, I petitioned the Lord, not only for a car with A/C, but also one with power steering. Jeanene, however, went a step further, as she asked the Lord to give me a nice car with an automatic transmission. At the time, I thought that was pushing it a bit, but on the other hand, why not? As usual, we ended the prayer by declaring those scriptures in John 14:13-14.

A few weeks passed before the insurance claim was settled. As it turned out, full coverage was retained after the Pinto was paid off. This was a miracle within itself, as Mother would normally drop such coverage whenever she obtained a clear title to any vehicle. With funds in hand, the car search commenced.

Mother ended up finding a late model compact car with relatively low mileage. It had A/C, power steering, and automatic transmission, which Jeanene had the faith to believe for. Mother, a wheeler-dealer when it came buying cars, could dicker with the best of them. She managed to get the car at a price I could afford. That "new" little red Pinto served me well for several years.

"Now all glory to God, who is able, through His mighty power at work within us, to accomplish infinitely more than we might ask or think." (Ephesians 3:20 NLT)

SUPERNATURAL PROVISION

The Lord knows college students live on a tight budget and pinch pennies for the most part. I was no exception. My junior year, I moved off campus, and was living close to school in a garage apartment. No curfews, no roommates, and the ability to practice at my discretion was liberating and a true blessing of the Lord. My piano had been moved to my apartment, which was an added bonus.

This new set-up came with increasing financial responsibilities, which meant I had to keep an even tighter rein on spending. I had to rely even more on the Lord. For extra money, I worked temp jobs during the summer, and sang as a paid soloist at funerals when requested. I was also a paid soloist/section leader at a local church, and once earned money by singing in the Fort Worth Opera chorus. That was usually enough income, combined with some financial aid, to get me from month-to-month; but there was not much wiggle room if something unexpected came up. Every once in a while, there was too much month left at the end of the money.

One Sunday morning, I remember driving to my church job, out of gas, and pretty much on fumes. To make matters worse, I was out of groceries at home. I didn't have a cent to my name, and payday was several days away. On the way to the church, I prayed for provision for the lean days ahead.

As I was praying, the Lord reminded me of His promise about provision. He said He would take care of my needs, so I did an about-face. Prayer turned into praise, and I began thanking God in advance for supplying the needed gasoline and food.

As I was walking to my car after church, I felt something stick to the bottom of my shoe. It was a $5 bill. That might not sound like much money, but back then, it was enough for a bit of gas and food, which sustained me until payday.

There was another time when payday was several days away, and the groceries just didn't quite last until the end of the month. Again, the Lord supplied the need, but in a different way. One evening, some friends from FOG came to my small apartment with a brown bag full of groceries. Now, I had asked the group to pray for my finances, but was too embarrassed to disclose that I was about to run out of food.

Regardless, I praised God and thanked them profusely, as they had been used by the Lord in an answer to prayer. Before I could continue expressing my gratitude, I was stopped in mid-sentence. They told me they were just delivering the food. God had spoken to someone else, who wished to remain anonymous, to bless my cupboards. Whoever that sweet person was, I asked the Lord's blessing on them. Jesus blesses those who give to others in secret.

I still get choked up when I think how the Lord used that person, who remained anonymous, to give so generously in my time of need.

"And do not be concerned about what you will eat or drink; do not worry about such things. These things dominate the thoughts of unbelievers all over the world, but your Father already knows your needs." (Luke 12:29-30 NLT)

A THOUSAND SHALL FALL AT YOUR SIDE

A crucial outreach of the church I started attending in my late 20's was short-term missions, some of which took place during the summer months. Such outreaches were in the U. S. and abroad. The trips could last for just a few days, or go on for weeks or months. One such mission trip was scheduled for Katowice, Poland, and the Lord impressed me to go. I felt strongly that if I stepped out in faith and signed up to go, God would provide.

Meetings to prepare for the upcoming trips began several months prior. Topics of discussion at the meetings varied from preparation for the outreach, defining our purpose for going, and fundraising. At each meeting, the outreach leader would go around the room, and get an update from each person on their status concerning such topics. Some gave very heart-wrenching reasons as to why they wanted to go on this outreach, while others did not elaborate. I had no deep reason, other than the Lord had impressed me to go, which was good enough for me.

From that point on, the meetings turned into teaching us how to prepare for the trip mentally, physically, spiritually, and financially. We were highly encouraged to send out letters to solicit support. It stands to reason that fundraising is the most logical route to take in order to pay for such a trip, but the Lord was not leading me to go that direction.

At the meetings in the weeks to follow, the leader went around the room to check on everyone's fundraising status. Not many had raised all their funds, but most had raised some. Of course, I hadn't raised any money. When called upon, I told him I had not raised any funds, and gave him this same answer the following few weeks. On the surface, it looked as though I was not taking the financial aspect of this trip seriously; however, the Lord told me He would provide. I was just waiting on Him.

"April showers bring May flowers" and sometimes, hail. In April of that year, a rainstorm accompanied by massive, softball-sized hail, pummeled the Dallas-Fort Worth (DFW) area. Damage from the storm was not only done to the property apartment buildings, but to vehicles. Hail decimated cars in the parking lot of my apartment complex.

Glass could be heard shattering all around the surrounding apartment windows, and the parked cars below. I was too scared to stay in my apartment, but it was unsafe to leave. The large hail sounded like bombs going off in a war zone, leaving a trail of debris mixed with precipitation.

As I saw my car being beaten to death by hail, I asked the Lord to protect the car windows. I didn't really care about the exterior, but please Lord - protect the interior, and save the windows and windshields! "A thousand may fall at your side, ten thousand at your right hand, but it will not come near you." (Psalm 91:7 NIV) came to mind. I proclaimed that scripture, but adapted it to the situation at hand. A thousand (hailstones) shall fall at 'my' side, and ten thousand at 'my' right hand, but it will not come near 'my' car windows.

The next morning after the storm had passed, I ventured out to the parking lot to assess the damage. Shards of glass and debris were scattered as far as the eye could see. Fortunately, my car was parked in close proximity to the apartment, so I didn't have to walk far.

As expected, significant damage was done to all cars in the lot, and mine was no exception. A window or two had been broken out of every vehicle I could see, but my windows did not suffer any damage - just as I had prayed. There was a smattering of hail dings on the car body, and a back tail light cover had been damaged. As soon as I could, I contacted my insurance company to file a claim. Although the car was paid off, I had retained full coverage.

The insurance company deemed the car a total loss, and gave me the option to buy it back—which worked to my advantage. In the negotiating process, I was able to buy my car back at a nominal price. The settlement gave me more than enough to pay for the trip. Although the body did not look great, the car ran fine, and I saw no reason to get rid of it.

God didn't cause the storm to happen in order to finance the Poland trip. Storms are part of nature, and bad weather is just going to happen. However, I do believe the Lord used the effects of that storm to my advantage – to pay for the trip.

At the next missions meeting, the leader opened with the same rhetorical fundraising question, but this time I was ready. I'm sure everyone was expecting the same answer from me as in previous meetings. This time when the leader asked if I had money for the trip, I answered with a resounding, "Yes!" No one in the room, especially the leader, expected that response. A few people did a double take, as I was the one expected to drop out.

Having said that, no one was ever rude, but since I had not raised a penny toward the trip prior to this time, it would stand to reason that I probably would not be going. To make sure he heard me correctly, the leader asked a second time about my fundraising status. I reassured him that God had provided all funds necessary for the trip, and then some. Then I told the group exactly how this miracle came about.

Several weeks later, I arrived in Poland with flute in tow. On the trip, we were able to reconnect with some old church friends, as well as participate in worship and small group outreaches—and to be a blessing to Katowice. It was amazing to be used by God in that way.

"God moves in a mysterious way, His wonders to perform; He plants His footsteps in the sea, And rides upon the storm." William Cowper (1731-1800)[1]

---

[1]Cowper, William. 1774. *God Moves in a Mysterious Way*. In *Olney Hymns*, vol. 1. Printed for W. Johnston.

CHAPTER 6

Hope for God's Will, Direction, and Career

HAVE WORK, WILL TRAVEL

The marathon of college was about to come to a close. With student teaching coming to an end and final exams and performances over, graduation was within reach. My next challenge was to get a job. I completed the course work to receive a Music Education degree in December, 1981.

There are usually not many (if any) job openings for teachers in the middle of the school year. My strategy was to work temp jobs until I secured a teaching position at the beginning of the next school term. Times were tough financially, so I moved back to Mother's house after graduation. The plan was to stay there just until I found a teaching job.

By June, I had submitted a plethora of applications to various school districts, but nothing panned out. Regardless, I had others agree in prayer with me. I kept my chin up, and was optimistic that something would eventually come up. It was around this time I had a dream where the Lord gave me a glimpse of things to come. In the dream, I was driving into the city limits of a small town. My car was packed, like I was moving there. It was a quick move, because school was just about to start.

In July, I got a call from a prominent school district located on the outskirts of Houston. The Fine Arts director offered me a job teaching junior high choir, and set up an appointment for me to meet with him. From there, we would go on to the district's personnel office to complete the necessary paperwork for hire. Since time was of the essence, I took off work and made the necessary travel arrangements in order to get to Houston in a timely manner.

I made arrangements to stay with one of my college friends for a few days to look at apartments. I packed to stay for several days. Since school was starting in a few weeks, I assumed I'd be in Houston for few days. Not only did I need to get the choir room ready at my new school, but I had to secure a place to live. I was giddy the entire trek down to Houston. Not only was I thanking God for my new job, but the fulfillment of the prophetic dream...or so I thought.

Bliss turned to utter disappointment when the director told me he could not hire me after all. He called me at home in Fort Worth to stop me from coming. Unfortunately, he waited too late to call, as I had already been on the road for a while by the time he called. This was way before cell phones, so I could not be tracked down.

Instead of reaching me, he ended up talking to my mother. According to the director, she had given him a piece of her mind. She showed no restraint as she told him how much trouble I'd gone through, for a job that did not exist. She was exactly right. The director had jumped the gun, by offering me the position prematurely. As it turned out, the choir teacher of that school had been on maternity leave.

She had previously told the director of her plans to resign in order to stay home with the baby. At the last minute, she changed her mind, and decided to keep her job instead. To add insult to injury, the director drove me to the school where I was promised the job, and gave me a tour of the choir room! It was a waste of time, money, emotion, and two days of my life I'd never get back.

Truth be told, I was frustrated with the teacher who changed her mind. At this point, I wanted to throw in the towel as I was tired of being disappointed. God had given me a dream, but I was struggling to see how He was going to make it happen.

"I would have despaired unless I had believed that I would see the goodness of the Lord in the land of the living." (Psalm 27:13 NASB 1995)

GOD WILL MAKE A WAY

Disappointment turned to unbelief, and I gave up. It was late July, and I should have secured a teaching job by now. The Lord knew how discouraged I was. A day or two after I returned from Houston, the Lord spoke to me in my sleep. This was not a dream or vision. The voice was calm and simply said, "Do not speak against the teacher (in Houston). She is wise to keep her job." As I woke up, I wept and repented for unjustly rebuking that teacher. If God wanted me to have that job, He would have given it to me.

I never thought I'd still be working temp jobs and living back at home so late in the summer. Mother thought the same thing, and she had grown impatient with my job status, as well. A few more weeks went by. By now, it was mid-August, and school was about to start. One day, Mother came in my room and gave me an ultimatum: Either get a full-time job locally (meaning apply at GD and work at whatever they offered) or get out. I went to my room, shut the door, and poured my frustrations out to the Lord, as I had done countless times before.

Just a few minutes later, Mother came knocking at my door. There was a person asking to speak to me from a school district, and they were calling long-distance. (Back in the day, you had to pay an additional amount of money to make a phone call to someone outside your immediate calling area. This was referred to as a toll or long-distance call.) Sure enough, it was the Elementary Music coordinator for Lufkin ISD on the line.

In a nutshell, the coordinator apologized for the late call, as the start of the new school year was within days. She explained that Lufkin ISD's school board had just approved two more music teaching positions for hire at the board meeting the night before.

As she interviewed me over the phone, she asked if I'd be willing to relocate to Lufkin to teach. I answered with a resounding "Yes!" Then, she asked if I could come down the next day to meet with the campus principal for an interview. I explained to her the debacle I'd just gone through in Houston, and she assured me that scenario would not happen again. Nevertheless, I proceeded with caution.

I had applied with Lufkin a few months prior, but never heard back, so I was surprised to get a call from them. I drove down, went through another interview with her and the school's principal, and was hired that day. I had to find an apartment and move quickly. Within a few days, I was teaching elementary music in Lufkin.

The dream of the late job offer, followed by a quick move came to pass - just as the Lord had shown me. God once again proved Himself faithful. He did exactly what He said He'd do, and only what He alone can do. God made a way where there seemed to be no way.

HOME IS WHERE THE HEART IS

Professionally speaking, Lufkin was great. I taught at one elementary school in the morning and another in the afternoon. Both campuses had wonderful full-time music teachers who mentored me. The second year, I was placed full-time at a brand-new school. It was the ideal district for me to really learn how to teach music.

I loved all faculty, administration, staff, and students in Lufkin. All went well for me job-wise; however, I struggled in my personal life, being alone in a small town. I didn't know anyone there my age. It was the kind of small town that, once kids graduated from high school, they left. Or, after they married and had children, they came back. There was not a "young singles" group in the Lufkin church.

Although I sought fellowship with a Christian college group in a town about 20 miles away, I didn't quite fit in as I wasn't in college anymore. By the middle of the second year there, I was extremely homesick, and found myself driving back to Fort Worth more often than not.

One night, I dreamed an angel was standing at the foot of my bed. I don't remember much about his appearance, other than he was wearing a white robe and had wings. He said, "Because you have been obedient, the Lord is sending you back home, and He is going to give you a job teaching junior high choir." This was the position I had wanted throughout college, prior to teaching in Lufkin. I was thrilled that the Lord was sending me home, but I told him that I wanted to keep teaching elementary music instead. The angel simply smiled and said, "OK!" Then I woke up.

HIRE THIS ONE!

After that dream, I began applying for teaching jobs in the Dallas-Fort Worth area. This time, however, I only sent out applications to the top five districts in the DFW area. It was different this time around, though. I had applied to these local districts before, and wasn't given the time of day. Now, I was able to pick and choose where I wanted to work. Experience made the difference.

There was one district in particular that was hard to get an interview with, let alone a job. At that time, the applicant-to-job ratio was fifty (plus)-to-one in Arlington ISD, as Bob Copeland, the district's FA Director, later reiterated. Nevertheless, I wanted to work in that district. Thankfully, I secured an interview with Mr. Copeland not too long after I submitted my application. In any event, the interview went very well.

At the conclusion of the interview, Mr. Copeland took the conversation in a different direction. He asked if I knew Charlene Watson. Everyone in the music teaching world knew Ms. Watson, as she was a recent past president of TMEA (Texas Music Educators Association). Needless to say, she had clout. At the time of my interview, she was teaching and serving as Arlington ISD's Elementary Music coordinator. I told him I knew who she was, but did not know her personally.

Apparently, Ms. Watson had influence when it came to hiring the district's music teachers. Mr. Copeland told me she had recently dropped by his office, for the sole purpose of looking through the applications for elementary music positions. He went on to say that, after Ms. Watson reviewed my application, she handed it to him and said something to the effect of, "She's a good one, she's from Lufkin. You need to hire this one." Lufkin ISD was well known amongst Texas music teachers for their exemplary music program. He told her that, coincidentally, he had scheduled to interview me the next day.

Whether Ms. Watson frequented the FA office randomly or on a regular basis, I will never know. I do believe, however, that it was the hand of God that guided her to find my application amidst all the others. What made my application stand out? Lufkin! Now it was all making sense. God never intended for me to work in Houston. The Lord's plan all along was for me to work in Lufkin, so I could be mentored, learn how to teach, and gain experience. Then, God made a way for me to go back home when the time was right.

Although I was extremely hopeful about the possibility of teaching in Arlington, I interviewed for (and was offered) jobs with other districts in the area, as well. When it was all said and done, Arlington ended up pursuing me. I signed a contract with AISD soon after tendering my resignation to Lufkin. God had provided once again.

"And the Lord is the one who is going ahead of you; He will be with you. He will not fail you or forsake you. Do not fear or be dismayed." (Deuteronomy 31:8 NASB)

CHAPTER 7

Hope for Love

LOOKING FOR LOVE
(IN ALL THE WRONG PLACES)

After I moved back home, I began attending an up-and-coming Charismatic church on the south side of town. This church's areas of outreach were on the cutting edge. I enjoyed singing on the worship team, and doing activities with the singles. One building on the church property housed a theatre where live, Christian-themed productions took place. The theatre was well known in Christian circles throughout the Dallas-Fort Worth area, as productions were constantly advertised on local Christian radio stations. There was always something going on at the church, and I immersed myself in those activities.

One Sunday afternoon, the church held a congregational meeting for members only. The pastor announced he was stepping down, as he had been involved in an inappropriate relationship. In the weeks, months, maybe even year that followed, the church faltered. Various leaders and pastors sought employment elsewhere.

As congregants left, ministries and fellowship groups began to consolidate or disband. It got to the point where I dreaded going to church, and finally made the decision to move on, as well. Unfortunately, I left feeling pretty disillusioned with the charismatic church, because of all that had transpired.

Soon after, I was invited by a friend to attend a mainline denominational church. My friend had gotten involved in the singles ministry at this new church, and urged me to do the same. I had nothing to lose, so I tagged along. Soon after joining the church, I joined the choir and started going to the Sunday School class where the singles gathered. Although I loved the church, I longed for the freedom and presence of the Holy Spirit I had so often encountered in the charismatic church. I started visiting a Spirit-filled church on Sunday mornings, but still did a few outings with the singles in the mainline church.

Loneliness can be exacerbated during the holidays. On Thanksgiving Day, one of the mainline single ladies hosted a dinner at her apartment. She also invited a few seminary students who had no place to celebrate the holiday. Even though I was transitioning out of the mainline church, I accepted her invitation.

At the gathering, I sat next to a guy who was a second-year seminarian. He had his sights set on going into the ministry as a vocation once he graduated in May. That was pretty much the long and short of our conversation. I doubted I'd ever see him again due to the fact I was in the process of changing churches. Wrong!

MR. WRONG

Mother always told me I would never be happy if I got married because that was her experience. Her relationship with Al had ended, and she found love again with her coworker, Paul. After a short courtship, they took a flight to Las Vegas and got married. By this time, most of my friends were either engaged or married.

The seminarian I had met at Thanksgiving got my phone number, called, and began pursuing a relationship with me. Even though I did not have a good feeling about it, I let my guard down, threw in the proverbial towel, and began seeing him.

He was a nice guy, but we were miles apart on spiritual issues. My walk with God was, and still is, deepened through the power of the Holy Spirit. It was hard for me to understand why someone would not want this same experience. The biggest point of contention between us had to do with speaking in tongues. We also differed in our expressions of worship. He practiced a more conservative approach, while my approach was less dignified.

Worship music at his church was beautiful and technically precise. After the song service, his pastor delivered a very cerebral, polished message. The seminarian would walk out of Sunday service feeling intellectually inspired, but it was just not my cup of tea, so to speak. I had been visiting a charismatic church in Grand Prairie, and it was beginning to feel like home. Their style of worship and sermons resonated within me.

When the Bible talks about being "unequally yoked," we usually think of a Christian marrying a non-Christian. In this case, the inequality had to do with the baptism of the Holy Spirit. He was not open to (nor did he want) any part of it. Whenever the subject was brought up, the conversation would always end in an argument. The Lord was making it obvious that he was not a good match for me, but I was not willing to listen.

"Do not be unequally bound together with unbelievers (do not make mismatched alliances with them, inconsistent with your faith)." (2 Corinthians 6:14 Amplified Bible)

I RAISE MY HANDS IN MY HEART

I never invited the seminarian to the Grand Prairie church, as I was well-versed in his opinion of Charismatics, and the Charismatic Movement as a whole. At this point, I was no longer willing to debate my faith, or the way I worshipped the Lord. As far as I was concerned, it was a mute issue and neither one of us was willing to change.

The Grand Prairie church hosted a worship conference once a year, and it was a "biggie." They pulled out all the stops, which included dancers and a smattering of free-lance tambourine players in the audience. Exuberant congregants also waved flags and banners in front of the podium - the works! It was like worship on steroids.

On stage front and center, there was a worship leader and his worship team that led the congregants in song. An orchestra that accompanied the worship team was positioned on one side of the stage; a choir on the other. The exuberant worship went on for quite a while. A church elder stepped up to a microphone on the side of the stage and gave a Word of Exhortation. What he said catapulted an already enthusiastic crowd to an even higher level of excitement.

As worship came to a close, the congregants took their seats. The senior pastor stepped up to the podium and asked all first-time visitors to stand up. In the section to my immediate left stood the seminarian, as stoic as ever. I acted as though I didn't see him. At the end of the service, I made a bee-line for the exit. He called me after work the next day to say he'd been at the conference the night before.

Even though I didn't ask him what he thought, he told me anyway. In a nutshell, he didn't understand any of it, especially the part about raising hands while singing. Although I knew any discussion was a waste of time, I went ahead to explain (once more) that I raised my hands as an outward expression of my love and surrender to the Lord. Before I had a chance to elaborate, he interrupted by saying, "I raise my hands in my heart!" I burst out laughing, as I could only imagine two little arms with tiny fingers protruding out of a heart!

He graduated from the seminary several months later. Since he couldn't find a ministry job in the DFW area, he ended up moving out of state and back home with his parents. The Lord had made it pretty obvious from the very beginning that this was not the right man for me. Now, God was taking drastic measures to end the relationship by moving him across the country.

LEANNESS TO MY SOUL

That night of his move, I dreamt I was in a huge high school football stadium. The stadium was crowded with people - all were dressed in white robes. They were cheering me on because the seminarian had moved. It was as if I had won some sort of game. When I woke up, there was no doubt in my mind that I had to break up with him. This scripture immediately came to mind: "Therefore, since we are surrounded by such a great cloud of witnesses, let us throw off everything that hinders and the sin that so easily entangles. And let us run with perseverance the race marked out for us." (Hebrews 12:1 NIV)

I made a long-distance call to him, determined to put an end to the relationship. Over the course of the conversation, he convinced me we could just be friends, which simply was not true. We kept the 'friendship' going for a few more months, even though I knew clearly it was not the Lord's will to even be friends. I was lying to myself by thinking I could reverse course, and go from having an intimate relationship to being casual friends. My desire for companionship overruled being obedient to the Lord.

I flew to visit him and his family during the Christmas holidays, and he told me he was coming to visit me on Valentine's Day. I knew what was coming next. In the weeks between Christmas and Valentine's, he sent me job applications from various school districts in his area.

The Lord could not have made it any clearer that this was not the one, especially after God had moved him thousands of miles away and given me the "Great Cloud of Witnesses" dream. Also, I did not love him; I just wanted companion-ship. Nanny always said, "If you don't love 'em before you're married, you'll hate 'em afterwards." I could not escape her wise words.

By this time, God, who is long-suffering, kind, and merciful, was out of patience with me, and gave me an ultimatum. One day, I opened my Bible, and this verse leapt off the page: "But they lusted exceedingly in the wilderness, and tested God in the desert. And He gave them their request, *but* sent leanness into their soul." (Psalm 106: 14-15 NKJV)

The Lord once told me, "I can lead people and I can show people - but I cannot make people do My will." God had led me back to a Charismatic church, and I followed. He'd clearly shown me this guy was not "the one;" however, the Lord was not going to force His will on me either. I'd get what I wanted (marriage) but at the cost of damaging my relationship with the Lord. Now I understood how easy it was to spiral down the wrong path, and continually make wrong decisions. Every time the Lord dug me out of the pit, I'd jump right back in.

Even when the Lord was giving me an ultimatum, He was still patient - like a loving father would be to a daughter. He showed me a glimpse of my future at the church in Grand Prairie. I saw myself involved in the music ministry there, playing flute in the orchestra and singing with the worship team.

My heart's desire was always to be a musician in the House of the Lord. Immediately, I broke down, sobbed, and repented. Later that day, I contacted the seminarian and broke up with him. I didn't have contact with him again from that moment on, and never looked back.

"But if you refuse to serve the Lord, then choose today whom you will serve…But as for me and my household, we will serve the Lord." (Joshua 24:15 NIV)

LAY IT DOWN

One time while attending church in Fort Worth, a woman I knew approached me and said, "The Lord tells me you are going to marry a man who has been divorced and already has children." WHAT?? The Lord certainly had not told that to me! Not only did I reject what she said, I started praying against it.

Having said that, my heart goes out to those who have lost a spouse, either through divorce, or even worse, death. When children are involved, the loss is even more devastating. I was raised by a single parent. If it had not been for the help of my grandparents, the situation would have been even more difficult.

When you're an older single (I was in my 30's at the time) the majority of your friends are married—some with a child or two. Their focus has shifted to each other and/or the kids. You envy them for being married, and some of them envy you for being single.

I was beyond the College and Career crowd, and an older singles group was hard to find…but God! Thankfully, I was surrounded by Godly women while going through New Members classes at the Grand Prairie church. They hosted events for older singles, and the focus was very God-centered.

The guest speakers at the first singles gathering I attended were Wayne and Bonnie Wilks. Wayne briefly spoke of their passion for Jewish ministry. Then, Bonnie told the story of her struggles of wanting to be married as an older single. That got my attention, as I could completely relate. Her story was similar to the one I had just gone through with the seminarian. As she concluded, she spoke of how the Lord called her to set aside, or die if you will, to the desire to marry.

The Lord called her to be His bride. I knew the Lord was asking me to do the same. The desire to be married had consumed me and become an idol. It caused me to continue dating a man that God made very clear was not the one. I had to lay that desire down and return to Jesus – my first love.

"For if you live according to the flesh, you will die; but if by the Spirit you put to death the misdeeds of the body, you will live." (Romans 8:13 NIV)

PLAY THE SONG OF THE LORD

I joined the Grand Prairie church choir and got involved in other areas of worship. When the choir was not on stage, I sang with the worship team when scheduled. A couple from New Zealand was hired as worship pastors about this time. They brought band and orchestra instruments, such as violins, flutes, and trumpets to the forefront of the song service.

Instrumentalists were encouraged to play in a more solo aspect during designated times in worship. Vivien, one of the new worship leaders, referred to this as playing "The song of the Lord." Word got out to Vivien that I played the flute. Before I knew it, I was playing my flute in the orchestra.

Back in the day, the orchestra didn't rehearse regularly with the worship band or vocalists. The orchestra would show up just a few minutes prior to the start of the service, get the music hand-outs, tune (if time allowed) and play along. It had been a few years since I'd played flute in a worship service, so I was a bit out of sync. Nevertheless, after a warm-up and a few scales, I prayed, then played.

Worship had not been going on for too long, when Vivien halted the singing, but kept the background music going. She spotted me in the orchestra, and in her New Zealand brogue, spoke into the microphone for all to hear: "Teresa, play the song of the Lord!" Surely, she wasn't talking to me, as this was my first day on the job!

Thinking she had made a mistake, I ignored her—but it was not a mistake. She said it again: "Teresa, play the song of the Lord!" As terrified as anyone would be if they were put on the spot in front of a thousand people, I took a breath and said a short prayer: "Oh, God! Help!" With shaking hands and a sweaty upper lip, I played the tune that came to my head. I knew the Lord had given me His song to play, as I was not smart enough to make a song up that quickly on my own.

The next Sunday, I sat in the congregation—at least that's where I started. All the musicians on stage were doing a quick sound check as the audience gathered in the sanctuary. Then I heard that New Zealand voice come through the sound system for all to hear: "Teresa, where's your flute?" I pointed to the exit behind me and responded, "In my car." I thought that would be the end of it, but it wasn't. She continued: "Go get your flute. Come play the song of the Lord!"

I retrieved my flute, sheepishly got on stage, and played with the orchestra. All the while, I was praying that I wouldn't be called out, as I had been the previous Sunday. Then, she did it to me again. At least this time she didn't call my name. She said, "FLUTE, play the song of the Lord!" The Lord was faithful to give me another melody to play. Looking back, I believe the Lord was prompting Vivien to have me play those spontaneous melodies. It was like on-the-job training, as the Lord was teaching me how to hear and play His melodies.

I played in the church orchestra for many years after that, and ended up playing more than singing when it was all said and done. Also, I must point out that Vivien had various instruments, not just flutes, play "The song of the Lord," as the Holy Spirit prompted her to do so.

"He put a new song in my mouth, a hymn of praise to our God. Many will see and fear and put their trust in the Lord." (Psalm 40:3 Berean Standard Bible)

FIRST BLOOD

It was May of 1993, almost a year after the Poland trip that God miraculously provided for. The worship pastor and his family that we served with in Poland had moved back home, and were ministering once again at the Grand Prairie church. He and his wife hosted a party at their home for the church musicians. During a game of Spoons, I became overzealous to stay in the game, and instead of grabbing the spoon, accidently scratched the competitor to my left. The scratch drew a bit of blood on the top of his hand. I was eventually eliminated, so I grabbed more snacks, sat on the couch, and watched the rest of the game. Also sitting on the couch was the guy whom I had injured.

Out of the blue, the pastor's teenage daughter blurted out, "You two are gonna get married!" Surely, she wasn't talking to me, and I didn't know that injured guy. That was a bizarre statement coming from a kid, and I blew her off. Now, I had seen the guy around. He was usually in the sound booth or singing on the worship team, but we didn't hang out with the same people.

Many months later, God gave me a "Song of the Lord" on my flute during Sunday morning worship. After the service, that guy came up to the stage while I was putting my flute away. He complimented me on my playing. After I thanked him, he continued to stand there, shuffling his feet as I quickly finished the task. Then, he looked up and said, "You wouldn't want to go out to lunch, would you?" I was actually meeting for an impromptu lunch with others, so it was no big deal if he wanted to come along. He decided to come eat with us, and from that point on became part of our group of friends.

A NEW RIDE

At this time, I was still driving my hail-damaged car. The exterior was by no means beautiful, but it got me from point A to point B. It had about 200 thousand miles on the odometer, and was beginning to be in the repair shop more often than not. Although repair costs mounted, I kept praying for the Lord to keep it running. It was nice not having a car payment for a few years.

Early one morning, the Lord woke me up and said I needed to buy a car. I shared my earthly wisdom with the Lord, telling Him I thought I was being smart by keeping the old car going. Apparently, God did not see it that way. After I told the Lord all of my reasons to keep the car, He reminded me of how many times I'd been left stranded for the last several months because of car problems. Above all else, the car was not dependable and had become unsafe to drive.

He also spoke something to me I was not expecting: "Buy the car now, because later your future husband would not understand, as he is more financially conservative." What a conundrum! I died to marriage so to speak, was not dating, and wasn't interested in anyone. The Lord's emphasis was on searching for a better car.

I began the car search, but nothing appealed to me. The cars I could afford were ugly, and I couldn't afford the cars I liked - so the search continued. Finally, the Lord told me to be specific in my prayer for a car, so I asked for a blue Pontiac, four-door sedan.

Luckily, at the time of my car search, they were giving teacher discounts at certain dealerships. The offer was about to expire, so time was of the essence. One Friday after school, I went to one of those dealerships, and ended up test driving a few cars with a salesman. None of the cars were what I wanted, but the salesman was anxious to close a deal.

He said he didn't have a blue four-door sedan, as that would have to be a special-ordered. Then, he remembered a shipment of new cars that had just arrived earlier that day. The new fleet had not been inventoried, so he had no idea what had come in. Just to humor me, however, he went to the back lot to check.

A few minutes later, the salesman drove me to the back lot, and there it was - a blue four-door sedan, just as I had envisioned. It was dusty on the outside, and the interior was still wrapped in plastic. After discounts, a price was reached that I could live with. They cleaned up the car, and I drove it off the lot that evening.

"Commit your way unto the Lord; trust also in Him, and He shall bring it to pass." (Psalm 37:5 NKJV)

DONUTS IN THE PARKING LOT

I drove straight from the car dealership to Fort Worth, to watch the Winter Olympics with my family. The women's figure skating finals were on TV that night. We were not die-hard ice-skating fans, but we, like most everyone else, were caught up in the Nancy Kerrigan/Tanya Harding "Skate Gate." After a few hours of watching the Olympics drama unfold with my family, I made the trek back to my apartment.

When I got home, I returned calls from messages left on my answering machine. The messages were from the guy who had come up to me at church a few Sundays before. "Where have you been?" he asked calmly. I told him about watching the Olympics with my family, which he believed.

Then I told him about buying a car, which he did not believe. Since we were both on the worship schedule for the weekend, I told him that he could see my car the next day at practice.

As promised, I showed him my car. He asked if he could take it for a test drive, to which I replied, "Only in the church parking lot". We went to the empty lot in the front of the church where he started doing a donut! "Are you crazy??" I yelled. He said he was making sure the car had good steering and handled well. Before he started the next donut, I made him pull over, stop, and I abruptly took my car keys back.

I was getting back in the driver's seat and ready to go home, when he hopped in the passenger's seat. He chuckled, apologized, then asked where we were going to dinner. "Nowhere!" I responded, as I intended to go home after that.

After a few more apologies, he convinced me to grab dinner with him. I knew things were not going well when we couldn't agree on directions to the restaurant. After we arrived, he admitted he was "directionally challenged." The next week or so, he invited me to the Omni Theatre in Fort Worth. We had ice cream and briefly dropped by to visit my mom, since we were in the neighborhood.

After our brief visit, we drove back to my apartment. As we sat in my car, he proceeded to drink my newly-opened cold can of Diet Coke in its entirety. Between sips, he told me how the Lord had called him to be a Levite priest. This guy was flirting with me, yet about to take a vow of singleness. Whatever!

We became run-around buddies. He fixed my computer and we went on a shopping expedition or two. We were on a worship team together, but were nothing more than friends. Since he had expressed his desire to be a Levite priest, which meant staying single, I thought I would support him in that decision.

I was still teaching, and attending a weekly single women's fellowship. Even though I had to lay marriage on the proverbial altar, that did not mean sitting around to cry about it. I stayed busy and was happy.

MR. RIGHT

I always listened to worship music and prayed on my way to work every morning. On one such occasion, the Lord manifested Himself in a way I'd never experienced. Suddenly, I felt His holy presence in my car. The Lord sent His messenger, perhaps an angel, to speak to me and said, "You are going to be married on June 18." Although I was driving, I instantly began weeping and thanking God. Then I asked, "To whom?" I could only imagine the angel rolling his eyes. Then he responded, "Who do you think?"

The person that came to mind first was my run-around buddy, Dale. How could this be? He was just my friend and he was going to be a Levite priest! Before I could wrap my head around what had just happened, that holy presence was gone. I did not share this encounter with anyone, and told the Lord—if this was indeed 'the one,' He needed to tell the guy.

Sometimes when the Lord gives you a prophecy or word, it is to be shared with the world. Sometimes it is not – or at least not until you have the peace to do so. When the angel Gabriel spoke to Mary about conceiving Jesus, he revealed to her how the whole scenario was going to unfold. She was wise not to share her angelic encounter at that moment. Had she spoken prematurely, she would have been stoned to death. At the appropriate time, Mary shared the encounter with her cousin.

Mary's cousin, Elizabeth, was experiencing a miracle of her own. Although she was well past the child-bearing years, she was within a few months of having a baby of her own. Joseph, to whom Mary was engaged, wisely wed Mary, after the Lord spoke to him in a dream to do so. He was discreet and did not advertise Mary's pregnancy.

Mary was extremely wise to not advertise what the angel Gabriel had spoken. Sometimes it is just best to keep quiet. I didn't tell a soul about the angelic visitation – until the Word came to fruition. "And blessed is she that believed; for there shall be a performance of those things which were told her from the Lord." (Luke 1:45 KJV)

It wasn't too long after my encounter with the angel, that I noticed a change in Dale's demeanor. He called one afternoon after work, but I was headed out the door, so our conversation was brief. In that short conversation, however, I noticed there was a softer, kinder tone to his voice.

He wasn't acting like my run-around buddy anymore, and he started pursuing me. As dating developed into courtship, I really got to know him – his likes, dislikes, and sense of humor. Dale's kind demeanor reminded me so much of my grandfather, Daddy D.

There were no arguments when it came to religion, as we both believed in the baptism of the Holy Spirit, and speaking in tongues. I began to fall in love with him. This time, I had total peace from the Lord, because Dale was "the one."

He had captured my heart, and I could tell that I had captured his, as well. We sat by each other at church, worshipped together, prayed, and went out with other singles. Looking back, it was one of the most joyful times in my life. Later, I found out that, soon after the angel spoke to me in my car, he took a little detour and stopped to talk to Dale at his job.

Dale worked in Midlothian, a small town located on the outskirts of the Dallas-Fort Worth area. More often than not, he was the only one in his office during lunchtime, so he often just ate at his desk. He also utilized that time to pray and read his Bible.

One day (according to Dale) the Lord made His presence known in a tangible way during lunch/prayer time. God's presence was so strong, that Dale was compelled to lay prostrate with his hands covering his face, on the floor. The Lord then spoke these words to him: "I am enlarging your heart for Teresa."

As Dale wept, God indeed opened his heart for me. After he told me all this, I just had to ask him if he still had plans to become a Levite priest. He shook his head, rolled his eyes, and we both burst out laughing. I took that as a "No."

Our courtship was rather quick. We went from being acquaintances, to casual friends, to "buddies," to two people who knew, loved, and were in love with each other. There was no doubt in either one of us, that the Lord had orchestrated our whole relationship from the beginning.

He started dropping hints about marriage, asking what kind of rings I liked. I had not been looking for wedding rings, so I had no answer. Also, he needed to take the lead on asking me to marry him. On the last day of March that year, he asked for my hand in marriage. My answer was unequivocally "YES!"

A JUNE WEDDING

A few days later, I called the church to see if June 18 was available. Unfortunately, it was not. As a matter of fact, the sanctuary was booked solid with weddings every weekend for the entire summer—and beyond. Most couples reserve the sanctuary many months prior, as summer is the peak time of year for weddings. I was advised to either schedule for the fall, or wait until next June.

In order to get on the schedule, I reserved a date in the fall, but requested the June 18 date as a back-up. If it happened to become available, I wanted to be the first to know. Although this is the date the Lord told me, the church schedule was not coinciding. Lyrics of a popular song at the time resonated in my heart: "Whose report shall you believe? We shall believe the report of the Lord!" In the natural, June 18 was off the table; but by faith, we began planning our summer wedding anyway.

About ten days later, I got a call from the church. They asked me if I was still interested in the June 18 date. A young couple who had reserved that date, decided they were not ready, and called off their wedding. When they cancelled, June 18 became available. I immediately called Dale to update him on the opening, then called the church back to reserve the date.

Dale Conkel and I were married on Saturday, June 18, 1994, just as the Lord had spoken. It was hard to fight back tears of joy, as I walked down the aisle at church—to take Dale's hand. All the years of disappointment and heartbreak just seemed to wash away at that moment. Dale was well worth the wait.

"My beloved spoke and said to me, 'Rise up, my love, my fair one, and come away. For behold, the winter is past; The rain is over and gone." (Song of Solomon 2:10–11, KJV)

CHAPTER 8

Hope in Difficult Times

AN UNTIMELY BIRTH

Dale and I didn't necessarily plan to have a baby our first year of marriage, but we did not prevent it, either. After all, we were in our thirties when we married, and really, there was no reason to wait. By this time, I had been teaching for almost thirteen years.

All my pregnancies were incredibly difficult. With my first born, I had high blood pressure, and was put on bed rest for several weeks before giving birth. Thank God, I delivered a healthy baby boy. After an excruciating labor, an epidural that did not work, and 3 hours of pushing, a healthy (and "a-chirping" as Dale would say) Benjamin Dale Conkel was born. He was the apple of our eye, the joy of our hearts. I retired from teaching school in order to be a stay-at-home mom, and began teaching private music lessons in my home.

Two years later, I was pregnant again. This pregnancy was also difficult. It seemed as though I was sick from day one, until the time I gave birth. A few weeks before Christmas, I mustered enough energy to wrap some gifts. I was listening to televangelist, Jesse Duplantis on TV as I wrapped presents. He was preaching on why bad things happen to good people, which caught my attention.

One evening in mid-December, I came home from church after an orchestra rehearsal. Exhausted, I rested on the couch. A few minutes later, my water broke. This was way too early, as the baby was not due until February 23rd. Needless to say, we rushed to the hospital, and I was immediately admitted—and put in a delivery room.

There were no doctors or nurses in the room when the baby was born. I felt her coming, and yelled for help. I had given birth to a very tiny baby girl with strawberry blonde hair. We named her Elizabeth Nell, after both our mothers. The room was filled with medical staff within seconds. Soon after her birth, she was transferred to the children's hospital in Fort Worth, where she was diagnosed with heart problems—as well as other issues.

We were devastated, as the doctor's report went from bad to worse. I had given birth to a sweet little one, but not given the chance to hold her, as she was transported very quickly. As I wept and poured my heart and soul out to the Lord, I petitioned God for her healing—as well as her life. The church stood in agreement with us in prayer, also.

We headed straight to Fort Worth after I was dismissed from the hospital. Church staff and family members were already at the hospital, awaiting our arrival. We all gathered in the hospital chapel to intercede for baby Elizabeth, as "O Holy Night" softly serenaded us in the background.

After everyone left, we went back to the NICU to stay with Elizabeth, as long as the staff would allow. I hadn't gotten much rest, but my post-partum condition paled in comparison to the reality of having a baby, and the thought of losing her. Ironically, when I got home, I could not rest. After a few hours of tossing and turning, I made my way to the living room so as to not disturb everyone else's sleep. There, I prayed for the Lord's peace, but I also asked for divine guidance.

The next day as I was walking through the corridor of the hospital, I looked to my left, and there sat a little girl in a wheel chair. She was about ten, had short blonde hair, and wore thick glasses. My heart ached as I saw her struggle to move and communicate. While it was His will for that little girl to persevere through disability, I knew He was telling me He had a different plan for Elizabeth. He was going to take her to her Heavenly home.

The next morning, we got a call from the NICU, telling us that Elizabeth's condition was rapidly deteriorating. They told us to get to the hospital immediately. We called the church to see if the pastor and some elders could meet us at the hospital, as we wanted to have Elizabeth Nell sprinkled in baptism, and dedicated to the Lord.

Tears flowed down our faces as we made our way to the hospital. Even though the news was not a surprise, it was still devastating to have to face her death. Our pastor, some elders, and our family gathered in the NICU for the sad, but brief ceremony. She passed away soon after. Sometimes the Lord does not answer prayer the way we want, and it ripped our hearts to utter the words, "Not my will, but Your will be done."

Christmas that year was overshadowed with grief and tears, but we had to keep going for Ben's sake. Eventually, the many tears and deep sadness subsided, but that didn't mean we had forgotten her. When I last visited her grave, I envisioned her greeting me at the gates of Heaven. I can imagine her being tall like the Conkel's, and having beautiful strawberry blonde hair.

The days, weeks, even months that followed were some of the most emotionally difficult times of our lives. It was tough even seeing infants (especially baby girls) in their mother's arms or in strollers. I cried constantly and poured out my sorrow to the Lord. God heard every cry, and comforted our hearts through family, friends, and His Word. I marvel at the cards, letters, phone calls, and meals that would come at just the right time. The Lord knew what we needed, and when we needed it.

"Then Jesus called for the children and said to the disciples 'Let the children come to me don't stop them! For the Kingdom of God belongs to those who are like these children.'" (Luke 18:16 NLT)

IT'S A BOY!

After baby Elizabeth's death, we went through genetic counseling. Tests concluded that the defects which ultimately led to her death were an anomaly. It had nothing to do with our genetics. We were given the green light to go ahead and conceive again, if we chose to do so. We talked about it, prayed it over, and decided to have more children.

When we told our extended family I was expecting again, they were not happy. At first, I was hurt by their negative reaction. Why weren't they rejoicing with us? They had just been on this emotional roller coaster with us when baby Elizabeth died, so I understood where they were coming from. We lost our baby. They lost a granddaughter, a niece. Baby Ben lost his sister. They were still heartbroken, and not ready to possibly repeat that whole scenario. On the other hand, I was not getting any younger.

We had done our due diligence through prayer and counseling, and we had peace about our decision. This third pregnancy had challenges, but things turned out differently this time. On February 22, Mark Christopher was born, weighing in just shy of 10 pounds. He was born one year almost to the day of Elizabeth Nell's due date, in the same hospital, the same delivery room. Mark's birth was a happy occasion, and our family was able to rejoice with us, instead of mourn.

The Lord gave us "…beauty for ashes, the oil of joy for mourning, the garment of praise for the spirit of heaviness…" (Isaiah 61:3 KJV)

THE REFERRAL

When Mark was a toddler, I noticed that he was not acting like Ben did at that same age. Mark was born with normal APGAR scores. He was walking and talking (as much as any other toddler) until he was about 18 months old. It was then that we noticed regression in his development.

At one point, he was forming words and starting to speak a few words, short sentences—then he stopped speaking. His tantrums surpassed that of a normal toddler. He would have meltdowns over any and (pretty much) everything.

Meltdowns became the rule, not the exception. He would even play with toys in an odd manner, and could sit for long periods of time being mesmerized by spinning the wheels of his toy vehicles. One time we left him with a babysitter. While we were gone, he had completely torn down the drapes in the formal dining room.

Excursions and social outings were exhausting, if not impossible. One early evening in October, I took the boys to a church Fall Festival with a few other friends and their kids. The costumes, noise, and crowd proved to be more than Mark could handle, and he went into full meltdown mode. Mark has always been a big boy, always in the top percentile in height and weight for his age group. Restraining him was not an easy feat. I had to protect him from hurting himself, others (including me) and church property.

With all the strength I could muster up, I managed to get Mark to the car, strap him into his car seat, and take him home. The other parents who had accompanied us to the festival, graciously took Ben with them, so he could enjoy the festivities.

The pediatrician ignored me over concerns about Mark's unusual behavior. I asked him for a referral to a neurologist, which he initially denied. Insurance would not pay for such visits without a referral. For the life of me, I could not understand why the doctor would not help Mark in this respect. I am not a medical professional by any means, but it stands to reason that with an early diagnosis of whatever disorder Mark had, he would have a better chance for recovery with early detection. Why was there such resistance from this pediatrician for help?

I remember one doctor visit in particular, where Mark and I were waiting in the exam room. It took every ounce of strength I could muster up, just to keep Mark under wraps. Begging for the aforementioned referral for the "umpteenth" time, the pediatrician looked at me, sighed, and said with exasperation, "Mrs. Conkel, if I give you a referral, it would be a waste of time."

He went on to tell me that Mark would eventually have to be "institutionalized." In other words, Mark could not be helped, and there was no hope for him. From that point on, the pediatrician was not dealing with a mild-mannered mom. The fight was on, and I did not leave the doctor's office until I had a referral in hand so Mark could get the help he needed.

The neurologist to whom we were referred, got the ball rolling. From that point on, we were able to start getting Mark tested fairly quickly. Hearing and vision exams were done to see if those might be contributing factors to his erratic behavior. Thankfully, those tests came back normal. After all was said and done, the diagnostician and neurologist came to the same conclusion: Autism with Speech Delay.

Our hearts sank when we were given the results, but at least we now knew what we were dealing with. We sought the Lord as to how to navigate through these uncharted waters, asking for guidance to the right specialists/therapists. We were contending for Mark's healing.

"Keep on asking, and you will receive what you ask for. Keep on seeking, and you will find. Keep on knocking, and the door will be opened to you." (Matthew 7:7 NLT)

ENLARGE YOUR TENT

After Ben was born, I continued to teach until the end of the school year, then tendered my resignation. To supplement the household income, I began teaching private music lessons in our home, instead. Students rotated in and out of our home daily.

Mark's disorder warranted a plethora of in-home therapists and other support staff. Our living room served as the parent-student waiting room. The boy's bedroom ended up being Mark's therapy room, at least until bedtime. This meant that Dale and Ben had no space of their own.

I began seeking the Lord for a bigger home, in order to accommodate the constant flurry of activity. Where to go, and how we were going to get there, was beyond me. I just knew that the current situation was not working. We definitely needed more space, but Dale was not convinced. He was (and still is) more frugal, practical, and the more level-headed one between the two of us. Whenever the topic of moving was brought up, Dale either avoided, or quickly dismissed the subject. A larger home meant a bigger house payment, so God's wisdom and direction was needed for a remedy.

God knew the situation, but I needed to tell Him nevertheless. His Word encourages us to pray specific prayers. The book of Matthew recounts the story of the blind men who encountered Jesus. He asked them what they wanted from Him, as if He didn't already know. Since He knew their need before they spoke, why did He ask them? Perhaps the Lord wanted them to verbalize their need as an act of faith.

The Bible encourages us to make our petitions known to God. We needed more space to accommodate Mark's therapy needs, Ben needed his own room, Dale needed a home office for work, and I needed a piano studio. What seems impossible for man is possible with God.

A few months later, some farmland near our home was being cleared for a new housing development. With model homes in place, the developer started selling lots on which to build single family residences. One model home in particular really caught my eye. It offered the rooms and additional space we needed.

One day, I drove out to the new housing development site, and with anointing oil in hand, I touched the ground where the homes were being built. Putting my faith to action, I reiterated to the Lord our housing needs, and started thanking the Lord in advance, believing that somehow the need would be met.

"Now faith is the substance of things hoped for, the evidence of things not seen." (Hebrews 11:1 KJV)

THE SIGN

Sometimes the answer to prayer is not a quick fix, but rather the long haul. Please understand, I don't view God as a genie, that if let out of the bottle, grants your every wish. First and foremost, when I petition the Lord, I ask for His direction. If I take matters into my own hands before hearing from the Lord, things usually do not turn out well.

Many times, God's answer is not what I expect. Sometimes, He gives me the peace in my heart to go forward with my plans; sometimes He does not. Other situations call for patience, as the Lord has to work out the details. If the Lord had impressed me to stop praying for another home, I would have dropped the subject, and waited for further instructions.

Our finances had improved greatly from the previous two years, which was the time I originally began looking for a larger home. The music studio was at full capacity, and Dale's salary had increased. He, however, was still not keen on the idea of building another home from scratch. The neighborhood I was praying about, was now full of new homes, and on the verge of closing out. As I drove past lot after lot in this new subdivision, "Available" signs were being replaced by "Sold" signs.

In the summer of 2003, we celebrated our ninth anniversary by treating ourselves to dinner out at a nice restaurant. After dinner, Dale asked if I wanted to go somewhere else, perhaps shopping or to a movie. We weren't in any rush to get back home. That was probably the wrong question for him to ask, as I requested to visit the "new" neighborhood. With reluctance, he drove down one of the streets that was pretty much built to capacity. I asked Dale what it would take for him to reconsider. "A sign!" he quipped back.

Those words had no more left his mouth, when I looked up and saw an "Available" sign on the lawn of a spec home, where we had just pulled over. The home was the same floor plan as the model home I desired. I pointed the sign out to him and said, "There's your sign!"

The next day, Dale brought up the idea of talking to the salesman in the model home. My heart sank a bit, when the salesman told us the house was not available after all. Someone else had put a contract on the home, but the sign hadn't yet been taken off the property. Instead, we went to "Plan B:" Put earnest money down on one of the few available lots left, with the intent to build.

A few days later, the salesman called to tell us the spec home had become available again. Apparently, the person who had originally put earnest money on the house, backed out of the deal. We were able to submit a new contract, and transfer the earnest money to the spec home.

How the Lord turned things around in such a short period of time was nothing short of a miracle; however, there was one stipulation: We had to sell our existing home within thirty days, in order to meet the terms of the contingency contract. Our existing home was put on the market immediately, and we prayed for yet another miracle.

Our existing home sold within the thirty-day time requirement, and within the range of our asking price. We closed on our existing home at one title company in the morning, and the spec home on the same day at a different title company, in the afternoon. A courier delivered the required equity money to the other title company, a few hours before we were scheduled to close. Again, this is another example of God working things out in His perfect timing. Not too long after that, we were in our new home.

"Now unto Him who is able to do exceeding abundantly above all that we ask or think, according to the power that works in us." (Ephesians 3:20 NKJV)

THE POOL

After we had been in our home a couple of years, we decided to put in a pool. The boys loved to swim, and both had been involved in swimming lessons since they were toddlers. Mark especially loved the water, but it was difficult to chase him around any kind of water park or public pool. Inflatable plastic pools didn't last long in the backyard, due to our German Shepherd's teeth and claws. If we were going to put in a pool, this was the time to do it.

One obstacle we faced was access to the backyard. The only way equipment could have access to the backyard was via the empty lot next door. Our home builder had already closed out, sold the model homes, and moved on. Another home builder had a few lots to sell before they closed out. One of those empty lots was next door to us. This would work to our advantage, providing the access sub-contractors needed, to get in and out of the backyard.

From the beginning, Dale, the kids, and I prayed for God's favor and blessing on this project. Permission to access the vacant lot next door from the builder was an answer to prayer. Then we prayed the lot would not sell until after the pool was finished. As long as the property remained unsold, we were allowed the necessary access. Once sold, however, the deal was off, no matter where we were in the process.

It is quite an ordeal to put in an in-ground pool. Permits have to be granted by the city. Rain and unpredictable weather delay the process. Sub-contractor re-scheduling, cancellations, or delays are not uncommon. Equipment, workers, and inspectors are constantly in and out of the backyard for weeks on end. Nevertheless, we continued to pray for the Lord's favor, and believed for the pool to be completed before the property next door sold.

If the Lord had not given us the peace to put the pool in, we wouldn't have moved forward. Looking back, installing the pool when we did was all done in God's perfect timing. Had we waited until the next summer to do so, the lot would not have been available.

Finally, the day came when the pool was complete. It was up to code, passed all inspections, and the backyard fence was secured back into place. Water, fun toys, and people filled the pool. Within days after its completion, the empty lot next door sold!

How good the Lord was, to hold off buyers until the project was completed. The family who bought the lot next door, ended up being wonderful neighbors and friends. In addition, when the pool company came out to draw the dimensions, they miscalculated, accidentally mapping out a larger pool than we paid for. When I pointed out the mistake to them, they chose to absorb the cost, and give us the larger pool. It was more trouble than it was worth to measure the dimensions again. What an extra blessing!

"Delight yourself also in the Lord and He shall give you the desires of your heart." (Psalm 37:4 NKJV)

CHAPTER 9

Hope in the Battle

YOU FIGHT FOR YOUR CHILD – NO MATTER WHAT

Mark was in a special education program before he started kindergarten. He continued in special ed, while simultaneously being mainstreamed into regular ed classes, as much as possible. Parents of special ed kids attend a barrage of meetings with teachers—either in person, or by phone. The child's educational and behavioral needs are addressed in an Individualized Education Plan (IEP).

IEP's are designed to protect special ed students, by setting up a custom environment in which each child can thrive in the learning environment. This document maps out a course of action, as to how these goals will be implemented. Once the IEP is signed by teachers, administrator(s), and a parent, it becomes a legal document, and cannot be changed on a whim. If any change is to be made to the IEP, another meeting must be scheduled. A new IEP is then put in place; the old one becomes obsolete.

Mark's IEP required that he have constant supervision—not only in the classroom, but during lunch and recess. This constant supervision was in place to ensure he was learning to the best of his ability. It was also designed to keep him safe within the ever-changing social environment of an elementary school.

The school began to slack off when it came to supervising him at recess. This failure resulted in him being beaten up on the playground by the class bully. I would not have known about the incident, but for one honest person who worked at the school. This employee showed me pictures which the nurse took of Mark's injuries.

When I confronted the special ed teacher about Mark's recess supervision, specifically the playground incident, she tried to sweep the whole thing under the carpet. It became blatantly apparent that Mark's IEP was being violated. Administrators on the campus level, and eventually up to the district level, did their best to silence me. As a mother, I was furious and wanted to do everything I could to protect my son. An injustice had been done to Mark, and they needed to be held accountable.

God was calling me to fight for my child. Initially, it was not my desire to get into a confrontation with the school, and I resisted such a notion. After all, I had taught in public schools for many years before Dale and I married. Also, I knew that fighting a school (or school district) would be a David and Goliath battle.

One day as I was praying about the situation at hand, my time with the Lord turned into intercession and travail. A very clear Word from the Lord resonated in my spirit: "If you faint in the day of adversity, your strength is small." (Proverbs 24:10 KJV)

A DAVID AND GOLIATH FIGHT

Righteous anger is justified by the Lord. That doesn't mean to go around and be angry at everyone all the time. When it comes to defending a child, however, especially one with special-needs, it's necessary to have that fire, that righteous indignation, in order to fight. Such was the case when it came to fighting the school (and ultimately the school district) for Mark.

Had I not taught in public schools, I would have been clueless as to the inner workings of a school district. I would not be familiar with their terminology - or what goes on behind the scenes, so to speak. Since I spoke their language, I knew that a parent could either be a teacher's greatest asset, or biggest headache.

I started out as an asset. However, when the school made a concerted effort to cover my child's injuries in order to protect the perpetrator, I became the latter. The perpetrator's mother had a reputation for intimidating teachers and threatening the district with lawsuits. As previously stated, I did not choose this battle - it chose me. After Mark was hurt, and the Lord spoke His Word to me, it was on!

The first battle was with the principal, who came after me with all her might. The principal summoned a few first graders into her office, to have them tell her their version of the playground incident—as if it were the Spanish Inquisition. She quizzed the children individually as to what they had witnessed at recess that day.

In her efforts to act as judge with a witness pool of six and seven-year-olds, she overlooked the real problem: Mark had not gotten, and was not getting, the supervision as specified in his IEP. Needless to say, the fight escalated to the top special ed administrator in the district. At that point, it did indeed become a battle like that of David versus Goliath.

Even though the Lord had called me to the fight, the enormity of the situation was overwhelming. Also, I had no idea at the time how this fight with the district would play out.

"A Psalm of David. Blessed be the Lord, my Rock, who trains my hands for war, And my fingers for battle." (Psalm 144:1 NKJV)

THE FIGHT BEGINS ON YOUR KNEES

How does one carry out orders mandated by the Lord? Will there be a light at the end of the tunnel? If so, how do you get there? After walking with the Lord through many difficult situations, this is what I have learned: Saturate your every move, every decision in prayer. Fine tune your ear to hear what the Lord is speaking to you at the moment. Get to know Him through His Word, the Bible. You will become accustomed to His voice.

Move when He says, "Move." Jump when He says, "Jump!" Don't move when He says to be still, and be quiet when He tells you to stay silent. Talk when He opens your mouth to speak. If you listen, He will tell you what to say, and when to say it. We are all human and make mistakes, but that doesn't mean you have to walk in fear while in the battle.

One Saturday morning before the recess incident took place, a heavy burden came upon me to pray, and I could not escape that unction. I had an overwhelming sense to get alone with the Lord and cry out to Him. It started out as weeping and travail, but morphed into spiritual warfare, praying boldly and loudly at times. I had no idea what I was praying about, other than it was intense warfare on a high level.

I did not stop praying until I was released from the burden, which seemed to go on for a long time. Looking back, I believe the Lord was having me pray in preparation for the battle that I was about to ensue. A few days after that time of prayer, the playground incident took place.

The school was concerned about protecting their reputation more than Mark's well-being, so the principal summoned the top special ed administrator in the district to intervene. I was called into the district office to discuss the situation with this administrator, who offered Mark more accommodations - if I agreed to drop the matter. What the administrator offered were services Mark was supposed to be getting anyway - one-on-one supervision. It was time to take the next step, and file a complaint with the state education agency.

A couple of months after filing a formal complaint with the state, I received a response back from them. They came to the same conclusion after doing their own investigation, and substantiated my complaint: Mark's IEP had been violated due to the district's negligence. This was a huge victory, as more often than not the agency will side with a school district, rather than the parents.

The agency required mandatory retraining concerning the supervision of special needs children. This retraining would be monitored by the agency, and applied to all schools in the district. In their opinion, if IEP's were not being followed in one school, they were not being adhered to throughout the entire district.

Not only was this a win for Mark, it was a victory for all special needs students in the entire district. Sometimes you don't know how the battle you fight will impact others. I felt that justice had been served not only for Mark, but for all special needs students with Autism in the district.

The day I received the "victory" letter from the agency, I looked out in my backyard where I had two Hibiscus plants that seldom bloomed. On that day, both plants were filled with beautiful red flowers like I'd never seen before, nor since. This was the Lord's tangible way of showing His favor.

"The Lord your God which goes before you, He shall fight for you…" (Deuteronomy 1:30 NKJV)

CHAPTER 10

Hope for Healing Church Wounds

THE CHURCH THAT HURTS

Raising a child with Autism is no piece of cake, and can be exhausting at times. Advocating for a special-needs child ranges from petitioning for the best medical care, to making sure his specific educational needs are met. The fight for such accommodations is continuous.

Those who have not raised a special-needs child often become armchair quarterbacks. Their expert advice is freely given on how you need to discipline your child. From their perspective, it is a matter of obedience. They have no idea what you and your family endures on a daily basis.

Autism is pervasive - it is not a one-size-fits-all disorder. One autistic child might display meltdowns via rocking their bodies back and forth, and/or flapping their hands. Another might scream, bite, or throw tantrums (meltdowns) in fits of rage. You never know what will push their button, as that button could be pushed over the slightest thing at any given moment. Mark did not rock or flap. His meltdowns manifested through tantrums. He was a big guy, which exacerbated the problem.

Mark's disorder affected the whole family. Social gatherings were challenging. Any change in routine or personnel, whether at school or church, would trigger a meltdown. Such was the case at our church, when the children's pastor was laid off and replaced by someone else.

From the time the new pastor took over, Dale and I were called out of the sanctuary, more often than not, to retrieve Mark from children's church. One day, the new pastor requested to meet with us, and we gladly obliged. She came to our home, and asked us to come up with a plan of action for Mark, including new toys and other manipulatives. She said she wanted him to be successful in children's church. I worked feverishly to get the requested plans and materials together, then met with this pastor a second time where we reviewed a new plan of action. With her approval, we were going to train the workers in the new plan, the coming Sunday.

That Sunday, I escorted Mark to his class. I was met at the door by this pastor, who informed me that, in order for Mark to attend class, I would have to be his teacher. She made it crystal clear that neither she, nor the workers, were willing to work with Mark.

From that Sunday on, Dale and I alternated in attending children's church with Mark. At least one of us could hear the sermon every other week, which was better than nothing. Needless to say, we were disappointed. The church that we loved so much was making us feel like a burden.

The straw that broke the camel's back was when a fellow congregant publicly reprimanded and humiliated Dale and Mark, at a church-wide family camp out. This person was outraged that Mark was putting too many logs on the fire, and angrily made his opinion known for all to hear. Dale didn't respond to this man. He and Mark just packed up and came home. After the church camp out incident, we knew the writing was on the wall. It was time to leave the church.

Of course, no church is perfect because people are flawed. Although filled with good intentions, the church does not have all the answers. Having said that, we saw no point in returning to this church anymore. It had turned from a place of refuge, respite, and hearing God's Word, to a place of rejection and public humiliation. Autism awareness was not as prevalent back then as it is today. We were judged as parents who could not discipline our child.

After we left, we joined another local church, where we stayed for a few years. This time, we hired an attendant to supervise Mark in children's church. This allowed Dale and I to attend Sunday worship services together again. Ben got involved with the youth group, which had their own worship service. It was a relief to be able to go to church without drama.

As previously stated, people are not perfect – and churches are not perfect, either. The new church had its flaws, as well. Due to financial difficulties, the church lost its building. Staff members and associate pastors - including the children's pastor and youth staff/pastors, began to leave.

As we began to ask the Lord for direction, Dale and I felt very strongly that it was time to go. Although we knew it was time to leave, we were clueless as to where to go. Over the next couple of weekends, we drove around looking at local churches, all the while praying for God's guidance. One Saturday night, the answer came. We heard the Lord say, "It's nice to visit the relatives, but now it's time to go back to your family." An unusual word indeed, but I knew exactly what that meant. It was time to go back to the church in Grand Prairie, which meant going back to our roots—so to speak.

Although we knew we had heard from the Lord, I dreaded going back. We had a lot of history with the church in Grand Prairie, but things had not ended well when we left. I had to work through unforgiveness and bitterness that I had harbored in my heart when we left. God gave me the grace to not only forgive, but release bitterness from past offences.

My reluctance quickly disappeared on our first Sunday back, as we were greeted with open arms. Familiar faces greeted us before we could get all the way out of our car. One couple even met us in the parking lot with hugs and kisses!

Our first service back equaled that of a family reunion. Even the worship leader, whom we had known for many years, spotted us from the platform as he was leading the song service. After the sermon concluded, he made a bee line to our seats to hug our necks and welcome us back.

By this time, Mark was a teenager and Ben was in college. Mark had grown up a bit, and settled down a lot. He was able to be in the sanctuary with us, but would quietly leave with his attendant, as needed. It didn't take long before we were asked to serve on the altar team, and then as altar captains. We enjoyed serving in the church again, and getting connected to a small home fellowship group.

"Then Peter came to him and asked, 'Lord, how often should I forgive someone who sins against me? Seven times?' Jesus answered, 'I tell you, not seven times, but seventy times seven!'" (Matthew 18:21-22 NLT)

CHAPTER 11

Hope for Autism and Finding Humor in Challenges

IT HAS ITS MOMENTS

Without a doubt, raising a special needs child is challenging. Thank God, it does have moments of comic relief. When Mark was diagnosed with Speech Delay along with Autism, I began praying that the Lord would give him the ability to talk. All other attempts to get him to communicate proved futile. God granted our request and Mark began to speak. As a matter of fact, once he started speaking, he became a chatter box with no "off" switch.

Sometimes what he says is down-right hilarious. Such times helped us persevere in the midst of fighting his battles and other difficult moments. It put things back into perspective, and reminds us that God is still with us, and He is faithful regardless of the circumstances.

It is impossible to remember, much less write down, all his antics - but here are some that come to mind: Mark wanted to go to see a certain movie, but Dale got wind that the movie had to do with reincarnation. When Dale confronted Mark about it, he replied, "No – it's not reincarnation – it's PG!"

After a day of Christmas shopping, I arrived home and started unloading gifts from the car to the house. Since Dale's car wasn't in the garage, I assumed he had gone somewhere with the boys. That wasn't the case, however. For some reason, Dale had parked his car out by the front curb.

Regardless, Mark was at the kitchen table when I walked in, so I asked him if he would go somewhere else in the house, as I couldn't let him see the bags already in hand. It would spoil the surprise. Later on, I found him alone in the piano room with the doors shut. When I asked him what he was doing in there, he replied, "Not looking!"

Other funny moments include the time I asked Mark, "Who made this mess of toys in the living room?" He said, "The cat did it." We didn't have a cat!

One day, I took Mark with me to get Ben's car serviced. While in the car, Mark kept covering his mouth and pinching his nose. When I asked Mark what was wrong, he uncovered his face long enough to say, "Ben's car smells like teenager!" He was right! The junk food scent, accompanied by a small pile of dirty jackets in the back seat, did indeed give off a teenager-like aroma.

Mark began to write and use social media as a way to interact with others. After seeing wedding pictures that a relative posted on social media, Mark commented, "And they are happies never after."

We always propose a toast at midnight on New Year's Eve, followed by a glass of non-alcoholic champagne, and would let the kids join in. Mark's New Year's toast was, "Happy New Year to all, and to all a good night."

"I'M ON THE NICE LIST!"

Christmas is a special time in our household. We didn't really say too much about Santa, as our emphasis is to celebrate the birth of Jesus - the real reason for the season. We were always in a dilemma as to how to handle Mark's insistence that Santa was alive and well. We were hoping he would eventually grow out of believing in the jolly old man, but that did not happen. As a matter of fact, the older he got, the stronger this belief became. One Christmas, it got to the point where we could no longer delay the inevitable. The truth had to be told. After all, he was about 14 and way too old for Santa.

Mark kept wanting to add more gifts to his wish list just a few days before Christmas. He asked me if it was too late to "place his order." I had already purchased all the gifts, and had no more to spend. Going out in the mad crowd of shoppers this late in the game was out of the question. I told him Santa's workshop was closed! Also, Mark was determined to set up a camera on a tripod, in order to video Santa coming down our chimney. He couldn't fathom how such a big man could fit through our chimney—with a sack of gifts in tow.

Things came to a head that year on December 23 at high noon. As Mark began to position the camera on the tripod by the stairs in order to video Santa's big entrance, I protested loudly. I told Mark that one of us (meaning Dale or myself) would break our necks if we tripped on the tripod, in route to the kitchen on Christmas morning. It was not my wish to spend the holidays in the ER. As Mark and I continued to banter back and forth, he became even more determined to video Santa's grand arrival.

At this point, I was exasperated with him. Finally, I blurted out, "Have you ever seen the Christmas wrapping paper in the closet?" "Yes," he quipped back, as he continued setting up the tripod. Then, I asked if he ever noticed that all the presents are wrapped in the same paper that's in the closet. He couldn't figure out where I was going with this line of questioning.

I couldn't stand it anymore, so I finally cut to the chase and asked him: "Who do you think Santa is?" While he was poised to rattle off a detailed description, I stopped him in his tracks. I raised my hand then said, "Look who the real Santa is!" I further explained that the parents are the ones who buy the gifts, and how Santa is just make-believe. In disbelief he responded, "YOU? NO! I'm on the Nice List! What the Hell!!"

ANOTHER DRIVER IN THE HOUSE

Mark has matured over the years. Although he gets upset when things don't go his way, the meltdowns have decreased substantially. He even began studying for his driver's permit. At first, I was against the idea of him driving. I was worried that he would actually get his permit. One day as I was praying, this simple Word came to me: "He who started a work is faithful to complete it."

Mark not only passed his written exam, he completed an adaptive driving course that was tailor-made for him. The next step was to pass the driving test, which he did with flying colors.

His birthday was just a few weeks away when he got his license. As we were coming home from the DPS, I told Mark that he was going to inherit his dad's car for his birthday. It was an older model car with high mileage, but still looked good and ran fine. We always gave the boys our older vehicles to drive when they earned their licenses.

He was excited about getting Dale's car. When we got home, Mark immediately headed for the kitchen. There he found a big paper grocery sack. Before I knew it, he had filled the bag up with all of Dale's belongings from the car. When I asked Mark what he was doing, he said, "I'm helping Dad get his stuff out of my car!"

Not long after he got his license, he was out driving when another car pulled out in front of him. Mark swerved to avoid an accident. He, along with several other drivers, honked at the reckless driver. When Mark retold the incident to Dale, he said, "Honking at that bad driver made me feel very patriotic!"

"And I am certain that God, who began the good work within you, will continue His work, until it is finally finished on the day when Christ Jesus returns." (Philippians 1:6 NLT)

CHAPTER 12

Hope in Seasons of Grief

MOTHER

Mom was proud of her kids and loved her fur babies. Full of life, she loved to have fun. The eternal optimist, Dorothy Nell was the life of the party, always had a joke to tell, and never met a stranger. Her parents were loving and supportive, and she was the apple of their eye. Unlucky in matters of the heart and continually battling health issues, she seemed to take it all in stride.

Mother had health problems throughout her life, but battled cancer more than anything else. The first cancer she fought was a carcinoma. She had an oblong, misshapen mole on her arm that would not go away, and did not have it examined in a timely manner. By the time she sought medical attention, the mole had already done some damage.

Along with the cancerous mole, the lymph nodes in her left arm had to be removed. This removal caused her to have a swollen left arm, hand, and fingers for the rest of her life. She was only forty years old at the time.

A few years ago, Dale had the same type of mole appear on his arm. It looked eerily similar to the mole Mother had, and I insisted that he see a doctor. Sure enough, it was a malignant carcinoma, and surgery for its removal was scheduled immediately. Thank God it was caught in time. Unlike Mother, the early detection stopped it from spreading any further.

A few years after this cancer scare, she discovered a lump in her breast, which ended up being malignant. I had FOG intercede in prayers for healing. Mother ended up having a mastectomy, followed by several radiation treatments. She got through the surgery and treatments with flying colors. I wholeheartedly believe the Lord can heal supernaturally, but I also believe He uses the skill and wisdom of doctors to heal. The Lord chose the medical route to heal her.

Mother was in her late 70s when a lump was discovered in her remaining breast. Another mastectomy was necessary. Chemotherapy was needed this time, and it came with some nasty side effects—one of which was hair loss. Despite chemotherapy, the cancer still managed to metastasize, and we received the dreaded news that she only had a short time to live. She kept a positive attitude through it all, and even mustered up the strength to celebrate Ben's graduation from high school with the rest of the family.

After everyone left Ben's graduation party, I was able to have a time of prayer with her. Dale and I anointed her with oil. We then sought and believed the Lord for her healing once more. We prayed that the Lord would extend her life, despite the circumstances. Mother wept, and agreed with us in prayer by saying, "Yes, Lord!" Although she was not a church-goer, Mother had accepted Jesus into her heart. She had seen first-hand the Lord's supernatural ability to heal.

God in His goodness answered Mother's prayer in true "Hezekiah" fashion.

The Bible tells the story of how Isaiah the prophet went to King Hezekiah and told him to get his house in order, as his days were numbered. The king then sought the Lord, asking Him to extend his life. The Lord heard the king's prayer, and added 15 more years to his life. In like fashion, the Lord extended Mother's life for 3 more years, of which we were grateful. She was able to enjoy a few more birthdays and holidays with the family. (My sister even took her to Las Vegas one more time!) Looking back, I believe the Lord really gave her 43 additional years. She could have succumbed to cancer at the age of 40, but the Lord allowed her to live to be 83.

"Hezekiah turned his face to the wall and prayed to the Lord...(then the Lord told Isaiah) Go back and tell Hezekiah, the ruler of my people...I have heard your prayer and seen your tears...I will add 15 years to your life..." (2 Kings 2-6 NIV)

HOPE IN UNCHARTERED WATERS

It was June, 2013, when we prayed for Mother's healing. I remember it well. As I mentioned before, it was the day of Ben's high school graduation. Three years later in June, 2016, Mother's health took a downward spiral. The cancer had returned and she was no longer in remission. In the hospital more often than not, she was too sick to handle her legal and financial responsibilities.

Paul, her husband, did not have the mental or emotional wherewithal to do so. As per her request, I became her Power of Attorney. This meant making sure all bills were paid, as well as overseeing the property managers of two rental properties. Fortunately, one of my sisters had expertise in property management, which helped greatly. She conveniently lived near our grandparent's old house, which was now the Fort Worth rental property.

Making the right decisions as I walked through a barrage of legal, medical, and family issues was overwhelming at times. Since all this was above and beyond my expertise, I needed Solomon-like wisdom. Having said that, it was an unprecedented time of getting clear direction (and sometimes) immediate answers from the Lord, in each decision that had to be made. The Lord was faithful to help me navigate through these uncharted waters - but I had to obey His voice every step of the way.

Although Mother was a record keeper extraordinaire, her filing system made no sense to me. I could not find the Fort Worth property manager's contact information anywhere, and time was of the essence. Overwhelmed with the situation at hand, I prayed a desperate but specific prayer: "Lord, I need your help. You know what I'm looking for, and You know where it is. Please lead me to it." Soon after, the Lord guided me to a file cabinet where the needed information was found, written on a manilla folder.

As I became more familiar with Mother's financial affairs, my eyes were opened as to how she was being taken advantage of, due to her age and illness. For example, the property managers of both rental properties were sometimes very late in getting the rent money to Mom - sometimes not giving her rent money at all.

One property manager had a track record of doing expensive, unnecessary work. He would then reimburse himself from the rent money he'd already collected. He'd tell Mother of said improvements after the fact, but she was too sick to confront him. His modus operandi was to buy the house as soon as she died.

In a phone conversation with this property manager, he asked me to give him "first dibs" on the property "when she passes." As far as I knew, my siblings did not know this manager or his motives. I definitely thought this guy was a "wolf in sheep's clothing." Needless to say, I informed him that his services were no longer needed – effective immediately, after he revealed his plan. Then, I hung up the phone.

The Lord had clearly revealed the unjust actions and intentions of this manager, and a righteous anger burned within my heart. God had given me the boldness I needed to fire him on the spot. The next day, I decided to go to the property, to update the tenants on the change in management.

As I pulled up to the curb, I saw an older gentleman speaking to a woman on the porch. The man was the (former) property manager. It was no coincidence that he and I had shown up at the rental property to talk to the tenant at the same time. It was the Lord's divine timing. I was able to introduce myself to the tenant, and tell her that my sister would be the new property manager. I also reiterated to the former property manager that his services were no longer needed, as he did not want to leave the property.

THE CABIN

The second property was the Cabin, Mother's beloved weekend lake house getaway in East Texas. The Cabin had been rebuilt with the intent of becoming Mom and Paul's permanent residence after retirement. They did live there for a short time, but when they moved back to Fort Worth, Mother decided to turn it into a rental property.

The property manager hired to oversee the Cabin was just the opposite of the overzealous Fort Worth property manager. This one would not collect the rent on time, and would not require the tenants to pay for damage done to the property.

I planned a visit to the Cabin, just to check its condition. Neither Mother nor Paul had been out there in a few years, as they trusted the manager to do her job. Mother had gotten word that there had been some damage done in the kitchen, but that was an understatement. A fire, which started in the oven, spread to the burners and ended up gutting the entire stove/oven unit. Apparently, it had been in this condition for quite a while. When I confronted the property manager as to why the renters hadn't paid for the stove to be replaced, she simply answered, "They just couldn't afford it."

Critters had torn up the lawn, as there were deep holes scattered throughout the yard. A company was hired to place cages throughout the property, to trap the vermin. When the company came to monitor the cages, they dis-covered the traps had been destroyed.

The tenants confessed that one of their children had damaged the cages, but their solution was to have the child save up, and eventually pay for, the cages to be replaced. Unfortunately, the critter catchers needed immediate payment to replace the irreparable cages. As I was exiting the property, a neighbor approached me and let me know that police often frequented these tenants.

I was not used to confronting property managers and tenants; however, I was angry with all the shenanigans that were going on, especially with my mother being incapacitated. The question that bombarded my mind was, at what point does tolerance end and restitution begin?

When the cages were destroyed, I knew the Lord had given me a clear answer. Who could possibly ignore wild animals literally running rampant and causing damage to a property? The time of tolerance came to a screeching halt, and I knew beyond a shadow of a doubt that the Lord wanted me to stand up and fight on Mother's behalf.

"I praise you, Lord! You are my mighty rock, and you teach me how to fight my battles." (Psalm 144:1 CEV)

LET HER GO

Early one July morning, the next month after her health really started to decline, I got a call from the hospital. Mother, who was in ICU, had gotten worse overnight. I needed to get to Fort Worth as quickly as possible. Ben drove as fast as he could through morning rush-hour traffic, as I began calling the family. My sister who lives in Fort Worth, and her family, were already there when we arrived.

Mom's breathing was labored, and she was not very coherent. After we had been in the ICU with her a couple of hours, the doctor and other medical staff ushered us to a separate room down the hall, for a consultation.

Cancer had ravaged her body, and she no longer had the strength to fight. All that could be done medically had already been done. The only option left now was to make her comfortable. The writing was on the wall as her time had come. Now it was just a matter of time before her eternal destination would be realized.

As a family, we came to one of the most heartbreaking decisions of our lives – to let her go. My prayers shifted from that of earthly healing, to asking God to give her a peaceful transition to Heaven. Her last remaining hours here on earth were peaceful, and we were able to surround her with our love as we said our final goodbyes.

Whether expected or unexpected, the death of a loved-one, especially a parent, is one of the hardest things in life to walk through. After she passed away, hospital staff allowed us to stay in the ICU with her as long as we needed. I stepped out of her room to cry alone, and gather my thoughts. Then, I called a few family members to tell them the sad news.

The Lord poured out His compassion in so many ways during the loss of my mother. A couple of months after her death, I saw her in a dream. She was wearing a beautiful white chiffon dress, and sitting on the floor. She looked like the pictures I'd seen of her when she was in her late teens.

Her hair had grown back, and it was a thick, beautiful light brown. "Oh, Tessie!" she exclaimed. "The music! The singing!" She was so happy, totally healed, and her face was glowing. Even though that's all she said, it was enough. How sweet of the Lord to give me a glimpse of my mother, in her glorified Heavenly body!

"Behold! I tell you a mystery. We shall not all sleep, but we shall all be changed…"

(I Corinthians 15:51 ESV)

PAUL

Dale was laid off from his job the same day Mother died. He did not tell me he'd lost his job until the day after, as he figured mother's death was all I could handle in one day. Factoring into this already mounting stress, was caring for my mother's husband, Paul.

Paul did not have a family of his own. His first wife died of cancer, and they never had children of their own. His brothers had preceded him in death, and he might have had extended family—but we never saw them until after he died. After Mother's passing, we became Paul's care takers.

He was still living at home when she died, and he was suffering from dementia. We knew he had some memory problems, but didn't know to what extent. She was fighting her own health battle, while simultaneously being his full-time caretaker. Most of our family did what we could to care for Paul, and keep him living independently. We soon found out, however, that he was not mentally or physically capable of living on his own.

He regressed quickly after Mother's death, and was constantly in and out of the hospital. We had to place him in a rehabilitation facility after his last hospital stay. Rehab would not release him to live alone, so we had to put him in an assisted living facility. The facility was very nice, and our family visited him constantly.

Late one night in December, a little over five months after Mother died, I received a call from my sister. She told me that Paul had been rushed to the ER. He'd had a heart attack and was unresponsive, but still alive. Once again, we met the family at the hospital, where medical staff ushered us into a hallway to give us more bad news. He had flatlined in the ambulance in route to the hospital - but paramedics somehow managed to get back a slight pulse.

His vital signs were weak, and we needed to make the decision as to whether or not to resuscitate him—if that were to happen again. I was allowed to go back to the trauma room where he was. Machines were surrounding him as he lay stretched out on the gurney. The only sign of life evident was a very weak pulse that could be seen on the heart monitor. Other than that, he was lifeless.

I held his hand and simply told him that I loved him, but that it was OK to go ahead and be with Mom in Heaven. Within a few minutes after leaving the room, he passed away. Even though we did our best to take care of Paul after Mom died, it wasn't enough. We could not fill the void in his heart that was left after she passed away.

Looking back, I see God's hand of provision during that season so clearly. While out of work, Dale helped shoulder the burden of Paul's care, at a time when Paul needed constant care. His care was a full-time job for the entire family. Dale's lay-off could not have happened at a better time.

He was drawing unemployment and getting severance pay, which sustained us financially. We were still able to pay both boys' school tuition, and all our bills on time. We lacked for nothing. Dale's severance came to an end about the same time Paul died. A few weeks after his passing, Dale got a job which came with a significant salary increase. When you follow the Lord, He might provide in ways you do not expect.

"…I am He who will sustain you." (Isaiah 46:4 Compassion Bible)

EXECUTRIX TIMES TWO

Mother and Paul died within 5 months of each other. They had separate estates, and I was executrix of both. The primary dealings of Paul's estate had to do with paying his outstanding and endless barrage of medical bills, funeral expenses, and handling his partial ownership of the Cabin.

I will never forget going to the courthouse to probate Paul's will. As I sat on the old, wooden benches outside the courtroom entrance, my attorney conversed with another lawyer, who was also biding his time. My attorney introduced me to his colleague, and in the course of their conversation, mentioned that this was my second time to probate court within a six-month period.

In jest he said, "She's a two-timer!" He was right! I was just getting a handle on executing Mother's will, and here I was—back in the same courtroom with the same judge for Paul's will. At least I knew what to expect this time.

Amongst personal belongings, the three properties were the greatest challenge. When my grandparents died, Mother inherited their house (the Fort Worth rental property). Since she was their only child, she retained sole ownership. Before she married Paul, Mother had paid off her small homestead. Of course, Mother owned the other half of the Cabin. Fortunately, none of the properties had a mortgage, which was a huge blessing. I didn't have to sell quickly, or be pressured into taking any low-ball offers.

At the time of their deaths, the house-flipping craze was in full swing. A barrage of realtors, independent flippers, and individuals started contacting me by any and all means possible. They wanted to purchase the properties before we were ready to put them on the market.

Dale is the one who dealt with all legal and financial matters in our family, including the selling and buying of our homes. My role was to accompany him to the title companies for the sake of signing legal documents, but that was about it. Real estate was not my field of expertise by any stretch of the imagination, and I needed the Lord's divine guidance more than ever.

Each property had its own unique set of circumstances. I would consult my siblings, but none of us could agree on anything at the same time concerning property sales. When it was all said and done, I was legally responsible for any and all decisions. The Lord led me in a different direction, as the situation warranted. This meant I had to decide whether or not to sell "as is," renovate, hire a realtor, or sell by owner.

Sometimes it was overwhelming to deal with so much all at once. In any event, I did not make a decision unless I had the peace of God to go forward. Peace was the umpire that navigated me in the right direction. When I got off track, my heart was unsettled - but the Lord was faithful to straighten me out.

"And let the peace (soul harmony which comes) from Christ rule (act as umpire continually) in your hearts (deciding and settling with finality all questions that arise in your minds, in that peaceful state)…" (Colossians 3:15 Amplified Bible)

UNFORESEEN LEGAL ISSUES

The first property for sale was the rent house in Fort Worth. This property was more sentimental to my sisters, than to me or my brother. I had a soft spot in my heart for this house until I had to deal with the property manager. That cured me of all sentimentality.

It came to the point that I needed to know the status of the properties—my grandparents' house, in particular. Also, I asked my mother before she passed, if Nanny and Daddy D had a will. If so, had their will been probated? I had no idea if the property had ever legally been put in her name, or if it was still in my grandparents' name. There had to be a paper trail on this property somewhere. She got quite irritated when I asked her about it, and said something to the effect of, "I took care of all that!"

From that point on, talking about properties became a mute issue, as she avoided the topic altogether. I figured I'd shut my mouth, and just let the chips fall where they may, as the old adage goes. Unfortunately, I found out after she died, that it had not been taken care of from a legal standpoint.

The only deed found was still in my grandparents' name. Additional paperwork proving Mother was heir to the property, was never found. I had to prove to the court that Mother was the only child of my grandparents, and my siblings and I were the rightful heirs, since Mother had now passed. Proving such heirship was challenging, as we could not go forward without it.

At times, the legalese and red tape I had to wade through to obtain such proof, was overwhelming. I prayed the Lord would help me keep my sanity, give me wisdom, peace, and perseverance. It took some time for things to work out, and my patience was put to the test once more.

When it was all said and done, I was able to prove that my mother was an only child, and the property now legally belonged to us. The title company had originally demanded notarized affidavits from people who had known my grandparents, Mother and her kids. After I submitted documents proving we were the heirs, and legally owned the property, the title company backed down. Without a doubt, the Lord allowed us to prevail. The situation turned to our favor in one phone call. I was then able to move forward with the sale of the property.

God's leading for this property was to sell "by owner - as is" without renovation. Since it was a rental, the house was in pretty good shape and code-compliant. There was no reason to sink more money into it, as it would not have significantly increased the property's value. Also, I had a price in mind that lined up with comps in the area.

"All wisdom comes from the Lord, and so do common sense and understanding." (Proverbs 2:6 Contemporary English Version)

CHAPTER 13

Hope for When Healing Doesn't Come

BEN

When Ben was born, we bought a video camera and recorded his every move – awake or asleep, it did not matter. All his "firsts" in life were also caught on film – first tooth, first roll-over, first step. Ben was dedicated to the Lord at our church, just weeks after his birth. That was memorialized on video, as well. Every parent cherishes these kinds of videos, but now these videos are particularly precious to us.

Ben was funny, quick-witted, animated, and ornery at times. He was extremely smart, graduating Summa Cum Laude from high school, in the top 25 of his graduating class. I made sure he was either in honors or dual-credit classes, as he was bored in regular classes.

He needed to stay busy, as idle time presented him the opportunity to become the class clown. That strategy worked for most of his classes. Regardless, he was voted Funniest Band Member both his junior and senior years.

Physically, he had the build, height, and light-colored hair like the Conkel side of the family, but his brown eyes were like mine. A beautiful child that grew up to be a handsome young man, Ben had a smile and laugh that would light up a room. The party did not start until he arrived. That was Ben!

He was a gifted musician in both piano and percussion, and could have gone much further in that direction—but that was not his passion. Having said that, he did play keyboard in small prayer gatherings at church when he was in high school. He played piano (when needed) in the high school band during concert season.

Regardless, he pursued science and graduated with a degree in biology from Dallas Baptist University - a well-respected private college not too far from us. He landed a job in pharmaceutical sales, and was consistently a top sales representative in his company. Ben was well-loved and very blessed.

When it came to driving, however, he had a "lead foot." Speeding tickets became a point of contention between us, especially during his high school years. He was working after school, but not making enough to pay for the fines in a timely manner. I encouraged him to ask the Lord for forgiveness, and seek His guidance for a strategy to pay his ticket. At this point, he knew better than to ask us for the money.

Ben sought the Lord, and the answer came just in the nick of time. He got a call to participate in a study, which paid enough to cover the traffic ticket. At the time, I was grateful, yet puzzled at this answer to prayer. As parents, our intention was to show him how actions lead to consequences, and in turn, get him to think twice before speeding. As I was explaining all this to the Lord, God gave me a different perspective.

Dale and I always taught the boys to rely on the Lord, to call on Him. He will always be there for them. The Lord told me that Ben did call on Him, exactly like we had taught him.

From God's perspective, this was not so much about teaching him a lesson, as it was about showing Ben the Lord's mercy and lovingkindness. I was truly taken aback by the Lord's response. After that, I did not question Ben's relationship with the Lord.

"God is our refuge and strength, a very present help in trouble. Therefore, we will not fear, even though the earth be removed, and though the mountains be carried into the midst of the sea." (Psalm 46:1-2 NKJV)

GONE

After he graduated from college, Ben got married, got a job in his field of expertise, and was able to purchase a home. Things were going well. In addition, his wife had just given birth to a beautiful baby. We were overjoyed!

It was in the fall of 2021 that he began to complain about feeling under the weather. He couldn't quite get over being sick. One Friday morning, he called and asked me to bring over some canned soups, crackers, liquids - anything that might settle his stomach. He was experiencing a lot of nausea, and this sickness had taken its toll on him. I made a run to the store and grabbed the requested items, then headed to his house. I parked at the edge of his driveway, where he was able to pick up the sack of groceries by his garage door.

Ben came out briefly to retrieve the sack and we talked for just a second, as I knew he needed to get back to bed. I blew a kiss to him, and told him I loved him. He blew one back to me, and said, "I love you, too, Mom." That was the last time I ever saw him alive.

The following Monday, he called me from his doctor's office. The doctor was sending him to the hospital as his oxygen level was low. According to Ben, this was supposed to be a brief, 24-hour hospital stay, in order to get things back to normal. Once his oxygen level was up and stabilized, he would be released from the hospital, start taking his prescriptions, and continue on the road to recovery. The first day in the hospital came and went, as did the second. His oxygen level took a downward spiral on the third day.

During this critical time, we were praying, and calling everyone to pray with us. We believe in the power of prayer, and we, as did others, stood in faith for Ben's healing. The second day, we ran errands for him, as he had requested. Since Ben's car was left at his doctor's office, Mark and I retrieved it so it wouldn't get towed.

As a gift to his brother, Mark washed Ben's car - inside and out. Mark said he wanted his brother to have a clean car to drive home, after he was released from the hospital. Ben was truly touched by his brother's act of kindness.

On the third day of his hospital stay, X-rays revealed his lungs had extensive damage from pneumonia. Prayer turned into travail, crying, and begging God to spare Ben's life. We were also encouraging Ben to rely and lean on the Lord.

Late that evening, Ben's wife called to update us on his condition, which was much worse than we thought. The doctor was going to put him on a ventilator, and that's about all we knew. Our conversation was interrupted as my daughter-in-law had to take an emergency call from the hospital. Ben had taken a turn for the worse. As Dale called pastors and friends for prayer, I screamed out to God, took my Bible and literally stood on it – crying from the depths of my innermost being – Lord, let Ben live!

There came a point that I could no longer utter another word. An eerie silence enveloped the living room. The time was 10:45 pm, according to the kitchen clock. I then closed my eyes, and in my mind, I could see the word, "**gone**" written in bold, lower-case letters. I couldn't cry, or even utter a sound. All I could do was sit on the couch, paralyzed by the word that had just scrolled across my mind.

A few minutes later, Ben's wife called to tell us the devastating news. Her exact words were, "He's **gone**."

UNPARALLELED GRIEF

I have lost parents, grandparents, and other close relatives and friends - but nothing even comes close to losing a child. Both of our children's deaths were a surprise. Baby Elizabeth Nell was born prematurely, only living a few days, while we got twenty-six years with Ben. Losing both children, even though one was an infant and one an adult, can only be described as a sorrow that is above and beyond compare - an unparalleled grief.

As gut-wrenching as Elizabeth Nell's death was, it pales in comparison to the depth of sorrow in losing Ben. My heart, soul, and entire being felt as if it had been crushed a million times over. It is a pain so indescribably deep that no one, or nothing can heal it—other than the Lord.

"(King) David started trembling. Then he went up to the room above the city gate to cry. As he went, he kept saying, 'My son Absalom! My son, my son Absalom! I wish I could have died instead of you! Absalom, my son, my son!'" (2 Samuel 18:33 CEV)

THE CHURCH THAT HEALS

When my mother, step father, and Dale's mother passed away, our Grand Prairie church family, including our church small group, organized meals for us. Dale's workplace also provided great meals and support. Few things in life are more difficult than losing your parents, even when the loss is expected. It was a great comfort to have that love and support.

When Ben was put in the hospital, the church body stood in prayer with us for his recovery. Word spread quickly of Ben's untimely death, and the church was the first to make sure that meals were provided, along with prayer and moral support.

The church was also there to walk shoulder-to-shoulder with us, through the unprecedented mountain of grief that lay ahead. Lay members and pastoral staff saturated us with love, friendship, a shoulder to cry on, and counseling as needed. We wouldn't have made it through that season of grief without them!

It has now been over three years since Ben's passing, and our church family is still reaching out with love and support. Individuals from the church have reached out through phone calls, or coming up after church to pray for us on Ben's birthday and/or anniversary of his death. They've also reached out to us on holidays, which can also be emotionally difficult to navigate through. The church's outpouring of love and support during this time also allowed us to totally release any and all hurts and wounds from years past.

I also have a different perspective of the situation we went through with Mark concerning the church. At the time, the church staff and workers were clueless as to how to cope with a special needs kid, such as Mark. They couldn't deal with it, because they didn't know what they were dealing with. I can now understand their apprehension.

The church is not perfect by any means, and if you are a member of one for any length of time, you will be offended by someone or something. Offences will come as long as we have breath in our body – as long as we live here on planet earth. But it is important to forgive. Forgiveness is hard, but it is key.

"Forgive us as we forgive others." (Matt. 6:12 God's Word Translation)

UNEXPECTED FORGIVENESS

At the time of Ben's death, relations with some of my siblings were strained over estate matters. Our conversations would end in disagreement—more often than not. I had to distance myself from some of them, in order to keep my sanity.

The day after Ben died, the silence broke, as all my siblings called and wept with us. They, along with their families, were grieving also. We lost our son and Mark his brother. The extended family lost their beloved grandson, nephew, and dearly-loved cousin.

My brother was in the ICU and fighting for his life, when he received the horrible news. The frailty of his near heart failure left him barely able to utter a sound. Unable to speak himself, he wept over the phone; but he was able to muster up enough strength to express his sorrow.

My sisters also called. Their voices were filled with grief, and both were unable to control the tears. As we grieved together, the Lord reminded me of my love for them, despite our differences. It was all water under the bridge now.

The long and short of the matter was this: Life is too short to harbor bitterness and unforgiveness. It's not worth it. Anyone can pass away without notice. No one is guaranteed tomorrow, much less another breath. It's too late to make amends after we die, so it's better to keep short accounts - forgive quickly, and go on with life in peace.

"To everything there is a season, and a time for every purpose under Heaven: A time to be born and a time to die. A time to plant and a time to uproot, a time to kill and a time to heal, a time to break down and a time to build; a time to weep and a time to laugh, a time to mourn and a time to dance…a time to tear and a time to mend, a time to be silent and a time to speak, a time to love and a time to hate, a time for war and a time for peace." (Ecclesiastes 3:1-4; 7-8 Berean Standard Bible)

IN DREAMS

There have been so many tears, so many unanswered questions over Ben's death. The Lord knows I've cried a river and struggled with an abyss of grief over his loss. I reiterate that the sorrow of losing a child, no matter the age of that child at the time of death, is indescribable. Individual and group counseling, as well as the support of family, friends, and the body of Christ, has helped us navigate through such uncharted waters.

All these things are good, and certainly contributed to healing that continues to this day. The key to healing for me, however, is to constantly bring my sorrows, grief, and heavy heart to the Lord. No matter how many tears are shed, God is there to catch every one of them. "You keep track of all my sorrows. You have collected all my tears in your bottle." (Psalm 58:8 NLT). Truly, the Lord knows our sorrows and is faithful to comfort whenever we call on Him.

One of the ways He comforts is through dreams and visions. For several weeks after Ben passed away, I would have dreams with the same recurring theme: I was always looking for Ben, but never able to find him. Perhaps this was my subconscious processing his death, and helping me face reality. I didn't attach any spiritual meaning to these dreams. Then, several months went by that I had no dreams about him at all.

Let me make myself clear: I don't ask the Lord to give me dreams or visions of my departed loved ones. There is a story in the Bible where King Saul was in a battle with the Philistines. He sought a medium who, through witchcraft, had the ability to summon the prophet, Samuel, who had recently died. Samuel did indeed appear to Saul, who delivered the Lord's Word to him, but it was not encouraging. It was a Word of judgment.

To add insult to injury, Samuel was perturbed at Saul for being called back from the dead (1 Samuel 28). If the Lord gives you a dream or vision of your deceased loved one, take it as His blessing and a source of comfort. It however, is not something I would pray for.

About ten months after Ben died, I dreamed Dale and I were in the foyer of our church. I was folding letters, getting ready to send them out. As I took a break from my letter-folding, I decided to walk around to the east side of the foyer, where I saw Mark. He was standing by a long, beautiful countertop made of onyx stone. The brilliant countertop was waist high, and had a slight curve to it. Mark was on the left side of the countertop, and he was talking to Ben—who was on the right.

Ben looked about 18 – like he looked his first year in college. He was wearing a white dress shirt with a white t-shirt underneath. This is odd, but I noticed 2 black pens in his pocket. He was busy, but smiling. At one point, he started chuckling at whatever Mark was telling him.

From a distance, I yelled to Mark, "There's Ben!" Before those words could reach Mark's ears, however, Ben disappeared into a doorway. I concluded that the doorway led to a room of sorts. Running as quickly as possible toward that doorway, I looked everywhere for Ben.

To my dismay, he was nowhere to be found, and my heart sank within me. Suddenly, a flash of light appeared, and there he was, right beside me! I was able to touch his arm - 3 times to be exact. Touching his arm felt as real as touching my own flesh.

I believe this is the meaning of the dream: The letters I was folding and preparing to send out, represent the work I am still doing here on earth. Mark and I were on the left side of the counter, which indicates that we're still on earth. Ben was on the other side of the counter. The other side of the counter is Heaven. Ben working behind the counter showed me that Heaven is a busy place, full of activity. Even those black pens in his pocket symbolized that he is working, being busy, even having some sort of assignment or duty to fulfill. Ben appeared by my side, and God allowed me to touch him.

I believe that encounter was not a dream; it was real. The Lord allowed me to touch my son, and to see him in his Heavenly body – young, happy, at peace, yet busy. I will thank the Lord, and embrace that brief encounter for the rest of my life. It brought so much peace.

"We are confident, I say, and willing rather to be absent from the body, and to be present with the Lord." (2 Corinthians 5:8 KJV)

A VISION OF HOPE

The second December after Ben's death was especially tough. It was even more difficult than the first Christmas without him. In addition to the intensified grief around the holidays, we were also dealing with some difficult circumstances, that were beyond our control. The situation warranted outside mediation, counseling, and guidance. It wasn't going as well as we hoped, and I was in the depths of despair.

I remember being so baffled, so broken after one particular counseling session, that I went straight from the car to my prayer room, as soon as we arrived home. Tears flowed as I cried out to the Lord. When words failed, I wept and prayed in tongues from my innermost being. I cried, prayed, and poured out my soul to the Lord, until I couldn't weep anymore.

Mark came in while I was in the midst of crying and praying, to ask why I was so upset. Not wanting to go into too much detail, I briefed him of the situation at hand. In his monotone cadence, he simply responded, "It sounds like we need a Christmas miracle." He then nonchalantly exited the room, and went about his business.

That evening, I made dinner, then went on to bed. My heart was still heavy with all that had transpired that day. Unable to sleep, and after having tossed and turned in bed for hours, I got up, went downstairs, and cried and prayed some more. I flipped through the pages of my Bible, in hopes of glancing at a verse, or some random scripture, that would alleviate the insurmountable pain.

In a last-ditch effort, I begged the Lord to turn the situation around. I prayed the Lord would give me a Word. One Word from You, O God – just one Word out of Your mouth, can change everything. I wasn't asking for a sentence, or even a scripture. I simply wanted a single Word. With that last tearful petition, I went back to bed.

I soon fell asleep, then dreamt that I was standing in a line of people, in a large room that looked like a big, white cafeteria. The facility reminded me of a high school cafeteria, except the lighting inside was much brighter (and much cleaner!). Standing about nine people in front of me in line—was Ben. He was wearing a pair of Ray Ban sunglasses. Sunglasses? Indoors? I didn't understand why he was wearing sunglasses indoors.

He was too far away for me to talk to him, and he didn't see that I was waiting in line behind him. Once again, I noticed he was laughing and joking with the people around him, and he seemed to be fascinated with those glasses. Also, he was wearing a white dress shirt, just as he was in the previous dream.

Standing in line to the right of me was a very tall fellow. Dale stands 6' 3", and this man was even taller than Dale, by at least a head or more. He had broad shoulders, and a physique like that of a football player. His hair was a beautiful blackish/brown color. The royal blue sweater he wore was smattered with yellow/gold cat hair.

At random, *praise reports* would be announced in the cafeteria, about people whom the Lord had healed, or of healings and miracles that were currently taking place. Shouts of praise would resound throughout the room when these good reports were broadcast. Everyone in the room was praising the Lord—except me. Instead of rejoicing with the others, I was silent. My thought was - the Lord didn't heal Ben.

While standing in line, the tall fellow, who I named the Cat-haired man, was talking to me, but I was not listening to him. Instead of hearing what he had to say, I was distracted by the fur on his clothes. It bothered me that he did not change his cat-hair/dander-laced shirt, before getting in line.

The next thing I knew, I was walking through the line with a brown tray in hand, and a server was scooping food on my plate. After I got my food and exited the line, I began scanning the room, looking for a place to sit. I spotted Dale and Mark sitting at a table on the far-left side of the cafeteria. There were a couple of empty seats by them, so I quickly made my way to them. By the time I got to their table, however, the seats had been taken, so I ended up sitting at a table across from the Cat-haired man. He tried to converse with me, but I was distracted, looking for a seat to come available by Dale and Mark.

I wanted to get away from the Cat-haired man. Finally, a seat did become vacant across from Dale, so I hopped up to snatch it. As soon as I picked my tray up to move, someone else beat me to it.

I attempted to get up once more, but I physically could not move. It was as if I had been glued to the chair. In a split second, the Cat-haired man, who was still sitting across from me, grabbed both my hands. His grip was so strong that I could not move at all, like I had become paralyzed.

I leaned over to his left ear, to tell him of my grief over Ben, but the words would not come out of my mouth. Then, I leaned over to his right ear, to tell him my grievances about another family member—but my voice froze before I could even squeak out a word! When I thought about it later, I wondered if this was the same muteness Zachriah, Elisabeth's husband, experienced when he encountered the angel Gabriel in the temple (Luke 1:20).

The Cat-haired man's strength was unparalleled to anything I'd ever experienced in my life. It was a supernatural strength – perhaps that of an angel. As he held my hands, he said to me in a bold and booming voice, "HOPE!!!" The split-second after he spoke that Word, the scenery changed. I was no longer in the cafeteria, which I now know was the Cafeteria of Heaven. I was surrounded by bright, white light. The power of that one Word though, was resonating through my entire being - HOPE!

As I started to awake, I was aware I'd had a supernatural encounter in Heaven, and with a Heavenly messenger. The Cat-haired man was an angel! My hands were still gripped in the same way as the Cat-haired angel (formally known as the Cat-haired man) had held them. As I began to process this experience, I could not hold back the tears, which were now streaming down my face.

"Why are you in despair, O my soul? And why have you become disturbed within me? Hope in God, for I shall again praise Him *For* the help of His presence." (Psalm 42:5 NASB 1995)

HE TURNED OUR MOURNING INTO DANCING

More than a dream or vision, and without a doubt, I had just experienced an encounter with one of Almighty God's Heavenly messengers. As I lay in bed, I tried to remember every detail, while processing the whole experience. Then, I began asking the Lord some questions.

Why did Ben have Ray Ban sunglasses in Heaven? Since Heaven is a place of perfection, and everyone there is in their perfect, glorified bodies, why would Ben have a pair of Ray Bans? The Lord answered, "Ray Bans were something Ben enjoyed on earth."

Why did the Cat-haired angel have yellow-golden cat hair all over his royal blue shirt? The Lord's answer brought even more tears to my eyes: "Because he (the angel) had been in the presence of the Lion of the tribe of Judah." Jesus Himself had sent one of His messengers, straight from the Throne Room, to give me HOPE - the one Word I asked for!

I gathered my wits about me, just enough to put on my glasses and make my way downstairs. Dale was already there, eating breakfast, getting ready for work. I attempted to tell him all that had just transpired, describing to him the Cafeteria in Heaven, seeing Ben, and the encounter with the Cat-haired angel. Tears welled in my eyes. I could not tell the whole story without intermittent bouts of choking up and crying. It probably didn't make much sense to Dale; however, he must have gotten the gist of it, as tears began to flow from his eyes before I was able to finish the story.

A few hours later, we received a miraculous answer to prayer - as Mark had so casually prophesied. Without a doubt, God had intervened. By the end of the day, the tumultuous situation we had been lamenting over, turned in our favor. The Lord changed our sorrow into gladness, and we went on to celebrate the rest of the holiday season with friends, family, and joyful hearts.

"You turned my mourning into dancing; You peeled off my sackcloth and clothed me with joy, that my heart may sing Your praises and not be silent. O Lord my God, I will give thanks forever." (Psalm 30:11-12 Berean Standard Bible)

PUT YOUR HOPE IN GOD

As long as I live, I will never forget that encounter with the Cat-haired angel in the Cafeteria of Heaven, and how the Lord sent His messenger to deliver the Word I desperately needed to hear. God turned our hopeless situation around, and changed the trajectory from that moment on. It later dawned on me, that the Lord has changed the outcome of many hopeless and impossible situations throughout my entire life.

The thread of His faithfulness is woven within my heart. I confess that I have faltered, and been disobedient at times. In certain situations, I've been over zealous, and have gotten in God's way. I've not waited for His timing, which really messed things up.

When I am stubborn and think I know how to work things out better than the Lord, I always fail. But God, who is a patient and loving Father, is always there when I call on Him. When I repent, seek His help, and let Him work things out, He is faithful to save and rescue.

He's there through life's triumphs, tragedies, and every other unexpected circumstance we face. Without a shadow of a doubt, He still answers prayer, and is the God of Hope!

"The Lord hears His people when they call to him for help. He rescues them from all their troubles. The Lord is close to the broken hearted; He rescues those whose spirits are crushed. The righteous person faces many troubles, but the Lord comes to the rescue each time." (Psalm 34:17-20 NLT)

"May the God of Hope fill you with all joy and peace as you trust in Him, so that you may overflow with Hope by the power of the Holy Spirit." (Romans 15:13 NIV)

Photos

Teresa – First Grade

Only Pic of Entire Family - 1962

Nell & Kids - 1975

Daddy D & Nanny

Al

Mom and Paul – Wedding 1989

Teaching -1992

Wedding Day – June 18, 1994

Benjamin and Mark – Christmas, 2007

Hawaii, 2009

Hawaii, 2019

About the Author

TERESA CONKEL was saved at the age of 13 during the Jesus Movement in the early 1970s. Born in Fort Worth, Texas she was the youngest of four children and raised by a single mother. Although her family did not go to church, she had a desire to know the Lord, even as young as age six.

Her mother recognized musical talent in Teresa early on, and enrolled her in piano lessons when she was in first grade. She also developed a love for singing during that time, and fondly remembers harmonizing with her mother and sisters in the car. While still in elementary school, she was chosen to sing in the select choir, and that passion for singing continues to this day. She also developed her skill at playing the flute. In her senior year, she was named Arlington Heights High School Outstanding Musician by her band/orchestra and choir directors.

In her second year of college, Teresa's gifts in music began to partner with her passion for worship. As she played and sang with groups of skilled, Spirit-filled, and like-minded musicians, a deeper understanding of hearing the Lord's voice through worship emerged.

For many years, Teresa has served as a co-altar captain of an intercessory prayer team at her church. She is also a firm believer of utilizing the "Gifts of the Spirit," according to 1 Corinthians 12:11. As the Lord gives unction, Teresa loves to "flow" in the prophetic and Words of Knowledge.

Teresa and her husband, Dale, raised two sons and have one grandchild. She still teaches a full studio of private piano students and enjoys spending time with extended family.

ingramcontent.com pod-product-compliance
ning Source LLC
bersburg PA
W071754120626
0CB00002B/791